ALFRED BUELLESBACH AND MARCUS COWPER

Battlescapes

OSPREY
PUBLISHING

ALFRED BUELLESBACH AND MARCUS COWPER

Battlescapes

A Photographic Testament to 2,000 years of Conflict

First published in Great Britain in 2009 by Osprey Publishing, Midland House,
West Way, Botley, Oxford OX2 0PH, United Kingdom.
443 Park Avenue South, New York, NY 10016, USA.
Email: info@ospreypublishing.com

A CIP catalog record for this book is available from the British Library.

ISBN: 978 1 84603 414 5

Page layout by Myriam Bell Design, France
Index by Alan Thatcher
Typeset in Perpetua
Originated by United Graphic Pte Ltd, Singapore
Printed in China through Worldprint Ltd

09 10 11 12 13   10 9 8 7 6 5 4 3 2 1

Front cover: The battlefield of Blenheim.
Title page: Prussian memorial near Verneville. This area was part of the battles west of Metz during the
Franco-Prussian war in August 1870.
Previous page: The prevalence of cemeteries is a good indicator of the intensity of the conflict in the Ypres
area of the Western Front. There are over 150 Commonwealth War Graves Commission cemeteries, as well
as numerous French and German sites and memorials.

For a catalogue of all books published by Osprey please contact:

NORTH AMERICA
Osprey Direct, c/o Random House Distribution Center
400 Hahn Road, Westminster, MD 21157, USA
E-mail: uscustomerservice@ospreypublishing.com

ALL OTHER REGIONS
Osprey Direct, The Book Service Ltd., Distribution Centre, Colchester Road, Frating Green,
Colchester, Essex, CO7 7DW
E-mail: customerservice@ospreypublishing.com

www.ospreypublishing.com

Contents

✥ Photographer's Preface

When you look at his face you would not think it was wartime. He is smiling, and does not appear exhausted at all. The old sepia photograph shows my great-uncle Leopold Halm among his comrades somewhere in France in 1917. He was a cook, and with his white apron it is easy to pick him out in the photograph. He trained to be a cook in Cologne before the war, and there was plenty of use for his cooking talents after the Kaiser called the men to arms in 1914. His life behind the lines came suddenly to an end in 1918 when he took part in the Spring Offensive. Within two weeks he was killed by shellfire, 25km south-west of Amiens. His parents were assured that he 'was killed on the field of glory' and 'did not suffer'. Since then his body has rested in French soil, together with those of 2,639 other German soldiers in the German military cemetery in Morisel, 454km from his home in the German Rhineland.

I visited his grave for the first time 25 years ago. Together with friends I made a trip to France and had a tour of the Somme battlefields before enjoying walking the cliffs of the Picardy coast. I had just finished school and it was something of an adventure as I was not able to speak French. At this time there were still border controls in Belgium and France, and it was still necessary to convert Deutsche Marks into Belgian and French Francs. A few years ago I visited the grave for a second time and there was no border control, not even a visible border, and thanks to the Euro there was no need to exchange currency. Twenty-five years had passed but, with the exception of the trees which now were much taller, little had changed in the cemetery. The real change had taken place outside the cemetery where, as in so many other towns, you could see the presence of international companies. Just on the opposite street to the cemetery was a German supermarket. The lack of border controls, the Euro and international businesses were things that made the cemetery appear even older than it is. The time when Germans travelled to France to fight a war where they killed and in turn were killed seemed very far away.

Opening the gate to that cemetery was like travelling between two separate periods of history, though the connection still remains. Europe has experienced enough bloodshed caused by war throughout history. Leopold's fate, and that of millions of others, was part of the long journey that ended with a modern and peaceful Europe. Today as a travel photographer I appreciate travelling with no border restrictions. During my travels I visit places like Morisel on the Somme, places where nations fought and many people died. These locations are not on normal tourist routes but lie in ordinary settings such as the peaceful countryside. If you do not know what happened here, you would do as most people do, and drive through the area without any knowledge of the events that took place in the

The Marmolada and its glacier was one of the most fought-over sections of the Dolomite front in World War I. As the highest mountain (3,343m or 10,968ft) in the Dolomites, the Marmolada provides extreme weather conditions with cold, snow and thunderstorms, which caused as many casualties as the fighting. In December 1916, a single avalanche killed 270 Austrians. To avoid both enemy fire and the threats of nature the Austrians created an 8km-long (five mile) 40m deep (130ft) network of tunnels and dugouts within the glacier itself.

past. Although a united Europe without borders is taken for granted by many, it has taken 2,000 years of war and conflict in Europe to reach this point. Battlefields are strong reminders of the value of a united Europe and these places should not only be remembered by military historians, but also by the general public at large. A shared awareness of a common history is needed for a European identity.

It was in this context that I developed the idea of this book, presenting photographs of former battlefields as landscapes. As a photographer I was entering a field that is normally occupied by historians and military experts. Furthermore I was dealing with historic events that are not visible any more. In contrast to other books that deal with historical battles, the power of this work does not come from military statistics, discussions about tactics or old photographs, paintings or documents. My work uses a different approach. Using only new photography and giving basic information, the aim of this book is to challenge the viewer's imagination. Looking at the flatness of the Danube Valley near Blenheim, it is possible to imagine how 100,000 men advanced across it towards each other. Standing in the middle of the dense Hürtgen Forest in Germany one is able to imagine why American soldiers never knew what was going on near them and why they were afraid of being shot at from all directions. The beauty of many landscapes stands in high contrast to the cruel events that took place on the ground. When you see the beauty of nature revealed in the photographs, it is hard to imagine what terrible events took place over these landscapes throughout the centuries.

Having decided to photograph battlefields, the first issues arose even before the camera bag was packed. Which locations should be in the book? My first research on the internet brought up almost 100 important battlefields in Germany alone. The Michelin Atlas for France provides a map showing the locations of more than 250 French battlefields. My original plan was to shoot no more than 25 battlefields in ten countries. To pick such a small selection out of 2,000 years of continental history may appear impossible from the viewpoint of a historian, but not for my needs. With 34 battlefields in 12 countries I found a selection that provides a balance of important historical and military events during the past 2,000 years. Out of these 34 battlefields, 25 were located in the founding nations of the European Union. All the battlefields were located in the middle of Europe, from southern Denmark to northern Italy, and from southern England to western Poland.

The battles were fought in very different kinds of landscapes within Europe. Some of the landscapes are now known more as holiday destinations than they are for their historical importance. But many of the battlefields are household names. During the research I became aware of how many of these battles are still

In the wood at Losheimergraben at the Belgian-German border. Losheimergraben saw action at the beginning of the Battle of the Bulge in December 1944. Two important roads intersect at Losheimergraben. At their initial attack the Germans saw resistance here in what became known as the battle of the Losheim Gap.

present in our culture. Many children learn for the first time about Alesia and Vercingetorix when they read the Asterix comic books. In school you read Shakespeare's *Henry V* and learn about Agincourt. In music you meet Leuthen or Waterloo. The Normandy beaches, the Ardennes and the bridge at Arnhem have all featured in major Hollywood movies. If you visit Paris the metro will bring you to the Gare d'Austerlitz or Solferino station.

Knowing the name of a battle does not mean you know exactly where the battle was. I wanted the photographs to show exactly where the action took place. But where was that? Battlefields can extend from a small field up to a vast area of hundreds of square kilometres. The task was to dig deep into the literature of the battle history, looking for maps and comparing descriptions from various texts. Without the availability of the internet, this task would have been impossible, as information about some battlefields was only available thanks to the work of local groups who published their knowledge online. However, some battlefields were described in extreme detail. The battlefield guide for the area of Operation *Market Garden* (the fighting around the bridges in Nijmegen and Arnhem during 1944) covered some 288 pages – more than most Baedecker's guides use to describe a major European city – while shops in the Somme area offer topographic maps showing the German and British front-line trench systems.

From my work as a stock photographer I knew that good research is crucial for photographic work in the field and is often the key to success. Doing extensive research helps to save time on location and enables one to concentrate on being at the right spot at the right time. Unpredictable circumstances, bad weather or fast-changing light conditions can force one to forget all existing plans and switch to an appropriate back-up plan. On location there is no time left to read history books.

But even the best preparation does not guarantee success. Very often the picture on the ground did not match the one derived from historic maps and other descriptions of the area. In some cases hills 'taken by our troops' were nothing more than a slight wave on the ground, or turned out to have no geographical significance at all. Thus the images created in my mind instantly vanished. In such cases I found myself in a featureless landscape where I quickly realized that photographing battlefields is not like photographing the

Grand Canyon. Taking photographs of battlefields has little in common with taking commercial landscape or travel photographs. Battlefields are related to historic events and therefore offer limited options when it comes to taking visually attractive photographs. Unlike commercial landscape photographs, the positioning of the camera must concentrate on the historic events first and the landscape second. What makes it more difficult is that, for the most part, battlefield locations are either in average agricultural areas, or in urban areas with a high density of population and visible infrastructure. Dealing with all these considerations made this project very different from other work I have done – but also extremely interesting.

The experiences on location provided other surprises too. At several battlefield sites there were many more interesting things to see than I expected. Relics, monuments or memorial stones: the visitor is confronted with interesting stories which ask questions or present other facts that one does not expect. I took additional photographs showing geographical features or points of interest.

The village of Illy, north of Sedan, France. This is the scene of one of the major battles of the Franco-Prussian War of 1870.

Many of these monuments shown in the book not only give information about the battles, but also show how the battles are viewed by history. In some cases these monuments tell more about their erectors than the events which they commemorate. Very often battlefields became centres of nationalism, national myths and identity. The defeat of Vercingetorix was forgotten for centuries but the Gallic leader rose as a star when France discovered its roots 150 years ago, and the battlefield monument of Alesia is more revealing of 19th-century French attitudes than those of the ancient Gauls. The giant staircase in Redipuglia is more a monument to Italian fascism than it is to the Isonzo battles of World War I. The lion at Waterloo that points as a warning towards France has become obsolete with the passing of time and the development of the French role as a driving force for a united Europe, emphasizing that it is not only military history but social and political history that is driven by the events that occurred on these battlefields.

This project started when digital photography made its breakthrough into professional photography. At the outset six- to eight-megapixel cameras were used. If you plan to fill double pages and also want to exhibit, then this resolution is not adequate. It was also clear that this project would take years, and during that time the digital world would make massive improvements. So I decided to get the best out of analogue photography and combine it with the benefits of digital post-production. I was looking for a large negative format providing the maximum resolution. I found the most suitable camera to be a Fuji G617. This camera provides a negative format of 6 x 17cm. It offers visual information almost three times that of the classic medium film format of 6 x 6cm and has a panoramic format with a ratio of 1:2.8. This camera has a fixed wide-angle 105mm lens, which does not allow long-range shots. This was another reason why the camera standpoint had to always be where the historic action took place. The benefit of the G617 is that despite its size it is not too heavy and it fits in a small camera backpack. Together with a light tripod, it can be transported even on long mountain hikes. On many occasions in the world of landscape photography you have to find a balance between equipment and mobility. There might be better cameras available but I did not want to limit my walking distance by carrying heavy tools. I used colour negative films in order to ensure all the detail was captured and available for digital post-processing. Negative films capture a wider

The Menin Gate Memorial for the missing of the Ypres Salient in Belgium. The Menin Gate, together with the Thiepval Memorial at the Somme, is the most impressive British memorial on the Western Front. It sits astride the road along which hundreds of thousands of troops passed on their way to the front and commemorates more than 54,000 officers and men who were lost in the salient.

range of contrast than slides. This matched my intention, as I did not want to photograph picture postcards in perfect light but average landscapes in average light conditions. This meant I had to capture hazy or overcast skies with high contrast. The smaller photographs in the book, with the exception of one on page 8, describing individual geographic points or tourist attractions, were taken with digital cameras.

Finally, I have to thank the Kulturwerk der VG Bild-Kunst in Bonn, which supported my project.

Alfred Buellesbach

✧ Introduction

The images in this book record the sites of over 2,000 years of conflict, from Caesar's conquest of ancient Gaul through to the final act of World War II in Europe, the Soviet storming of the defences of Berlin and the bringing to an end of Hitler's Third Reich. Throughout those 2,000 years, the shape of Europe's borders has ebbed and flowed as regional powers rose and fell, tribes and peoples moved and developed, and nationstates grew out of the early kingdoms of Europe in the face of both internal and external threats.

When Julius Caesar took up his governorship of the provinces of Cisalpine Gaul and Transalpine Gaul in 58 BC, the population of what is now modern France and the Low Countries consisted of a series of Gallic tribes, occasionally linked by trade or alliance, but essentially individual entities. It took the threat posed by the Roman conquest and occupation of much of ancient Gaul for these tribes to come together under their war-leader Vercingetorix and threaten the Roman hegemony; ultimately they were unsuccessful and Roman power eventually held sway from Italy all the way to the north of Scotland and as far east as the Rhine. The loss of three legions in the Teutoburg Forest in AD 9 left modern Germany and the Baltic states largely untouched by Roman conquest and influence.

The gradual collapse of the Roman Empire in the 5th and 6th centuries AD, in the face of the constant pressure of Germanic migrations from the east, left an absence of central control in Western Europe. In some regions, such as Italy and Southern France, the urbanized cultures remained much as the Romans had left them, whereas in others the Germanic incomers gradually took control and set up their own kingdoms – such as the Visigoths in Spain, the Anglo-Saxons in England and the Franks in France and Germany. These Germanic kingdoms faced a new threat from the 7th century AD with the birth of Islam and its rapid spread throughout the Middle East and North Africa. With the Muslim conquest of the Visigothic kingdom in Spain, the new religion had a foothold in Europe and it took a Frankish victory at Poitiers in AD 732 to push back the threat from the south.

The establishment of these kingdoms and the presence of the permanent military aristocracy required to maintain them, bolstered by the Catholic Church of Rome, led in AD 800 to the renewal of a western 'Roman' Empire with the coronation of Charlemagne, and the beginnings of the feudal system that was to hold sway throughout Europe in the medieval period. The conquest of England in 1066 by William of Normandy ensured that the British Isles would henceforth look more towards France and the Continent than towards Scandinavia, beginning a process of rivalry between the monarchies of France and England that would find its expression in the Hundred Years' War. This conflict saw large swathes of France fall under English control in the 14th and 15th centuries, and it gave the English the heroic myth of Henry V and Agincourt and the French the maid of Orléans, Joan of Arc. To the east, in what developed into the Holy Roman Empire, a series of important families gained control of the important territories: Austria, Brandenburg, Bohemia and Bavaria. These families, such as the Habsburgs and Hohenstaufens, would provide rulers for central and Eastern Europe for centuries to come.

It is these great dynastic families – notably the Bourbon monarchs of France and the Habsburg rulers of Spain and the Holy Roman Empire – that dominate the history of Europe during the Early Modern period up to the French Revolution. Following the tumultuous events of the Reformation in the 16th century, the growth of Protestantism and the Catholic Counter-Reformation backlash that followed inevitably led to warfare throughout Europe. Religious ideology led to wars of religion, initially in France (1562–98) and then in Germany with the Thirty Years' War (1618–48). The latter conflict in particular devastated parts of Germany to a degree never previously seen in warfare.

As these new conflicts dragged on, new powers rose: Sweden became the centre of a Baltic empire stretching into Northern Germany, and the Dutch provinces started to throw off the yoke of Habsburg rule and establish themselves as an independent trading state, while the late 17th century also saw the rise of Brandenburg-Prussia as a major power in northern Germany, a process that would continue throughout the 18th century. To the east, the Ottoman Empire had gradually conquered much of the Balkans and Hungary over the preceding centuries, but the sieges of Vienna halted their progress westwards and proved to be the high-water mark of their territorial gains.

The 18th century in general saw a continuation of the dynastic conflicts that had characterized the previous centuries, with the duke of Marlborough and Frederick the Great proving the outstanding captains of the age, as the Wars of the Spanish and Austrian Successions saw the development of standing armies and increased level of professionalism in drill, training and technology. The emergence of a modern, western-looking Russia under Peter the Great also highlighted the rise of another major European power, a rise which was emphasized by Russia's role in the Seven Years' War (1756–63) – a conflict that can claim to be the first truly 'world war'.

A ruined Italian barrack in a gothic style on the Torre Falzarego, part of the Dolomite Front during World War I.

However the wars of the 18th century had exhausted the French treasury. Financial crisis led to a social crisis, with the outbreak of the French Revolution in 1789 and the overthrow of the established Bourbon monarchy, which transformed the face of western Europe. The French Revolutionary Wars would see the crowned heads of Europe – principally Austria, Prussia and Great Britain – unite in an attempt to crush the fledgling Republic and restore the French monarchy. However, France survived and its greatest general rose to take control of the state, as First Consul to begin with, but later as Emperor Napoleon.

The Napoleonic Wars that followed (1803–15) saw fighting throughout the whole of Europe and beyond as the French instigated a new way of warfare – the nation at arms – using all the available resources of a nation to man the great armies that Napoleon Bonaparte led to victory time and time again. He oversaw the fall of the Holy Roman Empire and rewrote the map of Europe before the disaster of his invasion of Russia in 1812, combined with Prussian resentment and the bleeding ulcer of his Spanish campaign, brought together another coalition against France that forced his abdication. Even then there was time for one last hurrah in the Hundred Days campaign, which culminated in the battle of Waterloo of 1815, where the French defeat truly ended an era.

However, the nationalist fervour that Napoleon had unleashed throughout his empire would not be stilled. Throughout the 19th century the effects of nationalism can be seen in the rise of the French Second Empire under Napoleon III, the birth of Italy as a sovereign nation following the actions of Garibaldi and the battle of Solferino, and particularly in the machinations of the German Iron Chancellor, Bismarck, as he united the independent German states around the Prussian monarchy, a process completed with the foundation of the German Empire at the end of the Franco-Prussian War.

The nationalistic sentiments that were unleashed by the French Revolution and nurtured throughout the Continental and colonial conflicts of the 19th century

London Cemetery and Extension, High Wood. The third largest cemetery on the Somme battlefield, London Cemetery and Extension is so called because the existing battlefield cemetery was greatly enlarged after the Armistice and now contains the graves of 3,871 men, 3,112 of them unidentified.

came to fruition in the 20th century. A series of defensive alliances and arms races drove the principal powers of Europe into war in 1914, a war that they all believed could be won by élan and manoeuvre in much the same way as many of the 19th-century wars had been won, but which instead turned into a four-year-long bloodbath. The industrial and technological developments of the 20th century ensured that warfare would be fought on a different scale, with the destructive power of modern artillery blunting every major offensive until 1918, when the Germans came close to breaking the stalemate of trench warfare, and then the Allies successfully did so. World War I introduced the world to both the tank and aerial warfare, but it was World War II that was to see their development into war-winning weapons systems.

Born out of the ashes of the peace settlements of World War I, World War II was once again a war of ideology, as the monarchies of the early 20th century fell away and were replaced with one-party dictatorships: fascists, national socialists and communists, all with their own explicit agenda. The Germans appeared to have solved the conundrum of 20th-century warfare with their combined use of armour, artillery and aerial power to smash the Allied armies in the west during the 1940 campaign. But their attempted conquest of Soviet Russia exposed fundamental flaws within their armed forces, and the weight of Soviet numbers eventually began to tell, until eventually the Soviet armies stood on the river Oder outside Berlin. In the west, the Anglo-American alliance managed to move a massive armada across the English Channel to launch the largest amphibious landings in history, opening up a new front and driving eastwards towards Germany. It was a process that was delayed by notable failures in Holland, and German counterattacks in the Ardennes, but by May 1945 the Soviet and Western allies had defeated Nazi Germany.

The remainder of the 20th century saw no major conflict throughout Europe as the NATO alliance faced the communist-dominated Warsaw Pact countries across the 'Iron Curtain'. However, with the fall of the Berlin Wall and the collapse of communism in Eastern Europe in the late 20th century, the European Union has done much to integrate countries that were formerly enemies, putting in place structures designed to ensure that Europe is never again driven by warfare.

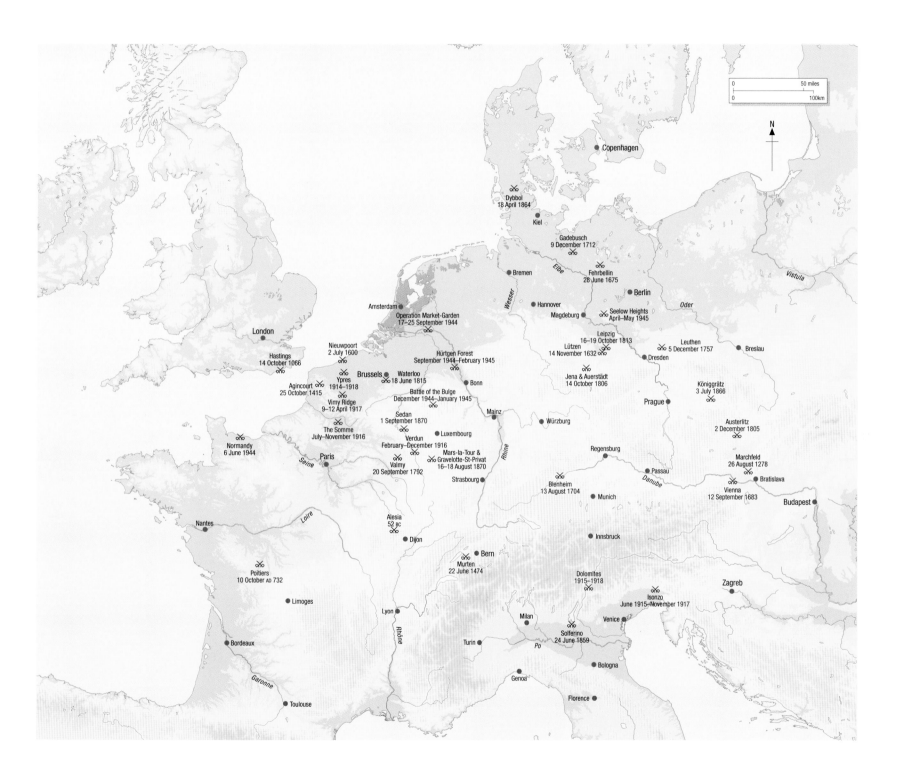

50 miles
100km

N

Copenhagen

Dybbol
18 April 1864

Kiel

Gadebusch
9 December 1712

Elbe

Bremen

Wesser

Fehrbellin
28 June 1675

Oder

Vistula

Berlin

Amsterdam

Hannover

Magdeburg

Seelow Heights
April–May 1945

London

Operation Market-Garden
17–25 September 1944

Leipzig
16–19 October 1813

Leuthen
5 December 1757

Breslau

Nieuwpoort
2 July 1600

Lützen
14 November 1632

Dresden

Hastings
14 October 1066

Hürtgen Forest
September 1944–February 1945

Brussels

Waterloo
18 June 1815

Bonn

Jena & Auerstädt
14 October 1806

Königgrätz
3 July 1866

Agincourt
25 October 1415

Ypres
1914–1918

Battle of the Bulge
December 1944–January 1945

Mainz

Prague

Vimy Ridge
9–12 April 1917

Sedan
1 September 1870

Würzburg

Austerlitz
2 December 1805

Normandy
6 June 1944

The Somme
July–November 1916

Luxembourg

Verdun
February–December 1916

Mars-la-Tour &
Gravelotte-St-Privat
16–18 August 1870

Marchfeld
26 August 1278

Seine

Paris

Valmy
20 September 1792

Regensburg

Passau

Bratislava

Rhine

Strasbourg

Danube

Vienna
12 September 1683

Budapest

Nantes

Loire

Blenheim
13 August 1704

Munich

Alesia
52 BC

Dijon

Innsbruck

Bern

Poitiers
10 October AD 732

Murten
22 June 1474

Dolomites
1915–1918

Zagreb

Limoges

Lyon

Isonzo
June 1915–November 1917

Rhône

Milan

Venice

Bordeaux

Turin

Po

Solferino
24 June 1859

Bologna

Garonne

Genoa

Toulouse

Florence

✛ Alesia

September 52 BC

This sign in the Oze Valley marks the probable location of the contravallation constructed by Caesar to prevent any Gallic relieving force from breaking through to the defenders of Alesia. This work duplicated the fortifications already constructed by Caesar to surround the Gallic hilltop fortress and remains one of the most striking Roman military engineering achievements of the period.

In 52 BC Julius Caesar finally completed the conquest of Gaul by routing the Gallic forces at the battle of Alesia. This victory finished the process begun when Caesar took up the governorship of the provinces of Cisalpine and Transalpine Gaul six years earlier, and ensured that Gaul remained a relatively stable part of the Roman Empire until its collapse in the 5th century AD.

Following his appointment as governor he undertook a series of campaigns, first against the migrating Helvetii tribe from Switzerland, and then against the tribes of the north-west, the Belgae and Nervii. In the following years he conquered the tribes in the north-east and on the Atlantic seaboard of modern-day France, and even found the time to cross both the Rhine into Germany and the English Channel to the British Isles. By 54 BC Caesar and his lieutenants had conquered all of Gaul; however, much of this conquest was only superficial. In the winter of 54/53 BC major revolts broke out, which led to the slaughter of the 14th Legion in the north-east. Although the region was pacified during the campaigning season of 53 BC, these rebellions were an omen of what was to come the following year.

In the winter of 52 BC an uprising broke out amongst a coalition of Gallic tribes led by the Arvenian noble Vercingetorix. Although the revolt started in the land of the Carnutes in the centre of Gaul, it spread throughout the country. The Gauls sought to avoid pitched battles with the Roman Army as

they feared the superior organization and fighting skills of the legions. Instead they waged a guerrilla campaign to wear the Romans down, although they did defend a number of their major hill forts and suffered a severe setback when

This statue of Vercingetorix stands on top of Mt Auxois above the town of Alise-Sainte-Reine. Designed by the noted architect Eugène Viollet-le-Duc, Napoleon III had it constructed in 1865, a time when nationalism was strong throughout Europe, in order to emphasize France's pre-Roman origins.

Caesar sacked the one at Avaricum. However, when he subsequently attacked the Arvenian hill fort at Gergovia, his army was defeated and were forced back with heavy losses, increasing the prestige of the Gauls' leader Vercingetorix and the potential success of the Gallic revolt. Vercingetorix therefore decided to stand and defend another of his forts, the important centre of the Mandubii at Alesia.

Caesar pursued him to the hilltop fort and laid siege to it, constructing a line of fortifications called a circumvallation to prevent the defenders from breaking out and being resupplied. These fortifications were staggering in their size and complexity, consisting of 18km (11 miles) of circuit featuring seven camps and 23 smaller redoubts, as well as a rampart, palisade and towers at regular intervals. In order to protect his numerically inferior forces against an attack from any relieving force, Caesar constructed another line of fortifications, the contravallation, facing away from Alesia.

These fortifications served their purpose and, although they came close to success, neither the Gallic forces inside Alesia nor a relieving force under Vercingetorix's cousin Vercassivellaunus could break the Roman siege. Seeing the futility of his position, Vercingetorix surrendered to Caesar and the 80,000 Gauls in Alesia were either sold as slaves or given to Caesar's legionaries as booty. Vercingetorix himself was ritually strangled following Caesar's triumphal procession in Rome in 46 BC.

The village of Alise-Sainte-Reine, Burgundy. Long believed to have been the site of the ancient battle of Alesia, the claim of Alise-Sainte-Reine has come under threat in recent years as arguments have been put forward for other sites, notably Chaux-des-Crotenay in the Jura region.

The village of Alise-Sainte-Reine nestling on the slopes of Mt Auxois, viewed from the west. This village in Burgundy, some 70km (43 miles) from Dijon, is believed by most to be the site of the ancient battle of Alesia. The photograph is taken from the point where Caesar's contravallation surrounded the Gallic hilltop fortification, preventing any relief army from breaking through.

Poitiers

10 October AD 732

On 10 October AD 732 a Frankish army under the command of the Mayor of the Palace and founder of the Carolingian dynasty, Charles Martel, defeated the Islamic Umayyad dynasty's invading force under the command of the governor of al-Andalus, Abd al-Rahman al-Ghafiqi. The exact location of the battle is uncertain, but it probably was near the hamlet of Moussais-la-Bataille, just north of Poitiers on the road towards Tours. For many years this has been claimed as the battle that saved Western Europe from Islamic conquest and, although this is overstating the significance of what was more likely to have been a major raid than an invasion attempt, it is certainly the battle that defines the high point of Umayyad penetration into Western Europe.

Following the Umayyad conquest of Visigothic Iberia in the early 8th century AD, the new province of al-Andalus began to push northwards. From AD 719–20 its forces began to conquer the region of Septimania, which stretched from the Pyrenees along the French Mediterranean coast, with the city of Carcassonne finally falling in AD 725. By this point, the Islamic forces had already ventured further north, as Prince Eudes of Aquitaine had defeated a substantial force outside Toulouse in AD 721, while another raiding party had pushed up the Rhône Valley as far as Autun in AD 725. However, having crushed an internal revolt, the governor of al-Andalus, Abd al-Rahman al-Ghafiqi, resolved to undertake a major raid and reconnaissance in force across the region

of Aquitaine, then an independent principality under Prince Eudes. The Muslim force crossed the Pyrenees in either May or June and proceeded northwards, meeting Prince Eudes in battle later in June outside Bordeaux where they

The modern village of Vouneuil-sur-Vienne is the closest centre to the probable location of the battlefield. The information board at this viewpoint provides details for visitors.

before the Islamic force attacked the Frankish position on 10 October. The Frankish infantry managed to hold off a series of frontal attacks and the Aquitainians under Eudes carried out a flanking cavalry attack that penetrated the Muslim camp, causing their main force to fall back to protect their booty. It was here that Abd al-Rahman al-Ghafiqi fell. The two sides drew apart and, during the night of 10/11 October, the Islamic Army withdrew in good order and began the long retreat back to al-Andalus.

There is an old Roman estate near the site of the battlefield called Vieux-Poitiers that may have been the location of the Frankish camp. Signs such as this lead visitors to the viewpoint.

defeated him before sacking the city. They then crossed the Garonne and defeated Eudes again at the junction of the Garonne and the Dordogne. It was at this point that Eudes headed for Reims to seek help from Charles Martel. In return for Aquitainian acknowledgment of Frankish sovereignty, and also to protect his own lands which were under imminent threat – particularly the abbey of St Martin at Tours – Charles agreed to assemble an army and march southwards. By September the Islamic Army had re-formed, following several months of pillaging, and marched northwards again, bypassing the city of Poitiers and heading for Tours. At the same time, the assembled Frankish and Aquitainian forces under Charles and Eudes had marched southwards from Orléans to protect Tours. The two sides met approximately 20km (12 miles) north-east of Poitiers, with Charles Martel settling his troops into a defensive position near the modern hamlet of Moussais-le-Bataille. There followed a period of stand-off between the two armies, perhaps for as long as seven days,

The battle is commemorated by a giant chessboard outside the village of Vouneuil-sur-Vienne, which explains the history behind the conflict.

The exact location of the battlefield of Poitiers is unknown, but most commentators hold its likely location as near the small hamlet of Moussais-le-Bataille some 20km (12 miles) north of Poitiers.

✦ Hastings

14 October 1066

The battle of Hastings, fought on 14 October 1066, was the decisive and only major battle of the Norman invasion of England. It changed not only the occupant of the throne of England but also the whole system of government, and brought a wholesale change in the upper echelons of English society.

With the death of Edward the Confessor on 5 January 1066, there were a number of rival claimants to the English throne. William, Duke of Normandy, had been promised the throne by his cousin Edward, while Harold Hardrada, the king of Norway, also had a claim as did Edgar Aetheling, a descendant of Edmund Ironside. However, it was Harold Godwinson, Earl of Wessex, who took the throne on 6 January 1066 as Harold II. He claimed that Edward had appointed him as heir on his deathbed and the Anglo-Saxon Witenagemot, a form of national assembly, supported his claim.

William of Normandy did not take the rejection of his claim without dispute and, having obtained papal sanction for his action, set about assembling an invasion force of his own vassals and of mercenary troops from throughout the French domains and beyond. Harold assembled his forces to defend his throne, but was distracted by the threat posed by his brother, Tostig, who had been deprived of the earldom of Northumbria in 1065 and had been attacking the East Anglian coast. In September Tostig joined forces with Harold Hardrada and landed an army just outside York, defeating the northern earls Edwin and Morcar at the battle of

Fulford Gate on 20 September, and occupying York itself. Harold marched his army northwards and defeated the Norse invasion forces at the battle of Stamford Bridge on 25 September, with both Hardrada and Tostig being killed.

The town of Battle in East Sussex stands on the site of the battle of Hastings. It grew up around the abbey of the same name that was founded by William in 1095.

Taking advantage of the English forces' absence, William had assembled his army and crossed the Channel on 28 September, establishing his force at Pevensey and Hastings on 28–29 September. Harold marched his troops southwards to meet him, mustering his army in London and heading south on 12 October, arriving at the battlefield of Senlac Hill on the evening of 13 October.

Battle Abbey was erected in response to a demand by the Pope for the Normans to do penance for the blood shed during their conquest of England.

The abbey was dissolved during the reign of Henry VIII, part of it now lies in ruins. The stone in the foreground marks the spot where Harold is believed to have fallen. (By permission of English Heritage)

William had a force of some 7,500 men, consisting of 2,000 horsemen, 4,000 heavy infantrymen and 1,500 archers and crossbowmen. To oppose them Harold had assembled around 8,000 men, consisting of around 1,500 of his personal household infantry and the rest made up of the assembled men of the Fyrd – the local militia. There were no significant numbers of cavalry or missile troops. Harold positioned his army on top of Senlac Hill in a solid shield wall, while William lined his troops up below him with the Bretons to the left, the Normans in the centre and the Franco-Flemish troops to the right. Following a barrage of arrows, William attacked with his infantry, which was beaten back by the Anglo-Saxon shield wall, causing William to commit his cavalry. However, they could not break the English line and the Bretons on the left broke and fled, leading a section of the English line to break the shield wall and pursue them. William's knights cut them down and the momentum began to swing William's way. The constant Norman attacks began to thin the numbers of troops in the English shield wall, and when Harold fell the wall lost its cohesion and the English broke, leaving most of their leaders, including Harold, dead on the field.

This view of Senlac Hill shows the ruins of the abbey in the background, with the dormitory to the right of the picture. The abbey now hosts a museum to the battle, set up and maintained by English Heritage. (By permission of English Heritage)

Senlac Hill, where the English shield wall lined up to face the Norman advance on the morning of 14 October 1066. An abbey was constructed on the site following the battle, and the hill forms part of its park. (By permission of English Heritage)

Marchfeld

The battle of the Marchfeld, also known as Dürnkrut and Jedenspeigen, was a dynastic struggle fought between Rudolf I of Habsburg and King Ottokar II of Bohemia for control of territory in what is now Austria. The Habsburg victory enabled them to build up the power base that led to them becoming the most powerful dynasty in medieval and early modern Europe.

Ottokar's father, Wenceslaus of Bohemia, took advantage of the crisis in German affairs caused by the deposition of Frederick II by Pope Innocent II in the Investiture Crisis of 1245 to take control of the duchies of Austria and Styria, appointing Ottokar as margrave of Moravia and duke of Austria and Styria. Following Wenceslaus's death Ottokar became king of Bohemia and attempted to secure election as king of the Germans in 1254, but Richard of Cornwall was elected in his place. Following a decade of conflict with the Hungarians over his territories in Styria and Carinthia, Ottokar once more contested an election for the throne of Germany, and this time lost to Rudolf of Habsburg, whom Ottokar refused to recognize. Following the Diet of the Realm in 1274, Rudolf ordered all imperial lands that had changed hands since the death of Frederick II in 1250 to be returned to the crown.

The river Morava (March) along whose banks the battle of the Marchfeld raged. The river starts in north-west Moravia and runs southwards, forming the border between the Czech Republic and Slovakia and then Austria and Slovakia before running into the Danube.

These lands included the duchies of Austria, Styria, Carinthia and Carniola controlled by Ottokar.

Following Ottokar's refusal to hand these provinces over, Rudolf assembled an army, besieged Vienna and forced Ottokar's capitulation in November 1276. Ottokar resolved to recover his lost lands and, having allied himself with Brandenburg and hired a substantial number of German mercenaries to bolster

his Czech troops, laid the towns of Drosendorf and Laa an der Thaya under siege. In alliance with King Ladislaus IV of Hungary, Rudolf's army set out to meet the Bohemians.

The plain of the Marchfeld. Ottokar's loss, and death, proved a significant setback for Bohemian ambitions, and from then on they focused on expansion eastwards at the expense of Hungary and Poland.

The two sides met on the Marchfeld, a plain next to the Morava River on 26 August 1278. Although, as with any medieval battle, it is difficult to judge precisely the numbers involved, contemporary commentators place over 55,000 men on the field, making it one of the larger battles of the medieval period, with the largest contingent being the Hungarian cavalry, many of them Cumans.

Ottokar drew up his army in six divisions: Bohemians, Moravians, Germans, two divisions of Poles and one of North German mercenaries. Rudolf faced him with three or four divisions of his own troops, plus another three Hungarian divisions to his left, all covered by a screen of Cuman horse-archers ahead of them. The Hungarian troops advanced, pushing the Bohemian and Poles back, while on the other flank Ottokar with his German mercenaries pushed Rudolf's force back. However, the commitment of Rudolf's reserve swung the battle his way, driving Ottokar's forces back into the Morova River, where many were killed. Ottokar himself was killed either on the battlefield or during the retreat that followed.

This memorial to the battle was erected on the Marchfeld by the villages of Jedenspeigen and Dürnkrut. Following the battle, Rudolf was able to consolidate his control over the lands in Austria, which then formed the bedrock of the growth of Habsburg power.

The landscape between Jedenspeigen and Dürnkrut where the battle took place. The wood in the background shows the location of the west bank of the Morava River. The fields of wheat highlight the fact that this area is the 'bread basket' of Austria.

Agincourt

Following a lull in major hostilities during the reigns of Richard II and Henry IV, the ascension of Henry V to the English throne in 1413 saw a renewal of English enthusiasm for war in France. Following a period of abortive negotiation, Henry mustered his army at Southampton in July and crossed over to France in August, with the aim of his expedition being the port of Harfleur in Normandy.

Henry's expeditionary force consisted of as many as 12,000 men. However, by the time that Harfleur capitulated on 22 September a significant proportion of them had been struck down by disease. Only 7,000 of the original force remained and Henry decided to march them across northern France to the British enclave of Calais.

The French had raised the war banner at St Denis on 10 September and mustered a substantial force, the advance guard of which was now sent to the river Somme to impede the English progress. The English Army set out on 8 October and, finding their route across the Somme blocked by a strong French force, they were forced to turn inland to find an undefended crossing. The English eventually managed to cross at Péronne, but by then the French main army had arrived and were shadowing the much smaller English force, eventually blocking the English path to Calais at the village of Agincourt on 24 October.

Henry deployed his troops in a defile with woods protecting both of his flanks. His main body of men-at-arms was in the centre, flanked by two contingents of archers protected from the French cavalry by stakes. Opposing him was a French army of some 25,000 men deployed in three 'battles',

These archers line the edge of the battlefield of Agincourt. Although the French also fielded archers in their forces, the English longbowman remains one of the iconic figures of the battle of Agincourt and the Hundred Years' War in general. Their intervention in the mêlée at Agincourt had a significant effect upon the outcome of the battle.

the English men-at-arms in the centre, while the English archers attacked them from the sides and rear. The first French battle was pushed back onto the now-advancing second battle. Following three hours or so of fighting, the English had won the day, though this was not clear to the English commanders. The presence of the sizeable French third battle, still uncommitted, combined with the sacking of the English camp by a sortie from Agincourt Castle led Henry to order the slaughter of thousands of prisoners taken during the battle, with only the most prominent being spared.

Casualty figures are difficult to estimate for any medieval battle, but it is clear that the French suffered serious losses. With many of the great names of the kingdom either killed or captured, the aristocracy was hit particularly hard. The English under Henry V were now free to consolidate their gains in successive campaigning seasons in Normandy.

This crucifix marks one of the French burial grounds. Although numerous men-at-arms died at Agincourt, it was the loss of so many members of the French aristocracy that was to cause problems for a generation. The Constable of France, three dukes, five counts and 90 barons fell on the battlefield, while many more were captured.

This table of orientation is situated at the rear of the battlefield, near the village of Maisoncelle. This was where the English drew up their battle lines in the early hours of 25 October 1415 before advancing towards the French lines.

one behind the other. The first unit consisted of men-at-arms, archers and crossbowmen, and included many of the great nobles of the realm. This first battle was flanked by two significant cavalry forces. The second battle was smaller and consisted of mainly men-at-arms while the third contingent contained the bulk of the French mounted troops.

Following a period of inaction in the early morning, the English advanced to within arrow range of the French first battle at around 11am and began to fire at them, provoking a charge by the two flanking French cavalry units. The weather had been extremely wet and their charge over recently ploughed ground lacked momentum and was disrupted by the English arrow fire. The French cavalry were eventually driven back to their own lines where they crashed through the advancing first French battle, creating disorder and confusion. The French advance pressed on through the mud and engaged

A view of the battlefield from the English perspective. The French line was situated in line with the house with the red roof seen on the right-hand side. The English advanced to this position at around 11am on the morning of 25 October and opened fire on the French, provoking them into a rash charge that set the scene for the rest of the day.

⊹ Murten

22 June 1476

The battle of Murten was the decisive battle of the Burgundian Wars of 1474 to 1477, fought between the independent duchy of Burgundy under Charles the Bold and the Swiss Confederation. Charles the Bold's defeats, primarily at the hands of the Swiss pikemen, caused the fall of his dynasty and the integration of the duchy of Burgundy into France.

The Burgundian Wars had their origins in a decision by the Habsburg Duke Sigismund of Austria to assign his lands in Alsace to Charles the Bold in an effort to secure them from the Swiss Confederation. When Sigismund made peace with the Confederation and sought to acquire his Alsatian lands back, Charles refused and Sigismund entered into an anti-Burgundian alliance with the Swiss and several independent Alsatian cities. The first year of the war saw Swiss victories at Neuss, Héricourt and Planta, the last against the Burgundian allies in Savoy. Charles retaliated by marching on the castle of Grandson on the route to Neuchâtel and Bern. Using his heavy artillery he battered the garrison into submission, and when they surrendered he had them all killed. The Swiss assembled a relief army and encountered the Burgundians outside Grandson. An attempted feint retreat by the Burgundians turned into the real thing and the Burgundian Army abandoned the field, leaving behind their heavy cannon but with little loss on either side.

Following his defeat Charles reassembled his army and once more tried to threaten Bern, reaching the town of Murten on 9 June 1476, which they

put under siege. The siege lasted until 18 June when the Swiss Confederation massed an army of 25,000, accompanied by 1,800 mounted troops under the duke of Lorraine, to oppose the Burgundians. Charles positioned his army behind a series of earthworks and palisades known as the 'Grünhag'. On the

Standing on the route from Payerne to Bern, Murten was a natural target for Charles the Bold in his campaign against the Swiss Confederation.

The town of Murten sits next to the lake of the same name, while to the north and east are wooded slopes. Charles the Bold set up his army to the south-east of the town.

The town of Murten had been fortified from as early as AD 100, and the ring wall that surrounds the city, which was built following a fire in 1416, remains one of the best-preserved and well-known fortifications in Switzerland.

morning of 22 June the Swiss launched a surprise attack on these defences while they were only thinly manned. Despite taking heavy casualties from the Burgundian artillery and English longbowmen positioned there, they broke through and were able to drive Charles' poorly organized forces out of his camp and back towards the shores of the lake, where many of them were drowned. At the same time the Swiss defenders of the town broke out, trapping the Burgundians' Italian allies and destroying them. Altogether the Burgundian forces lost some 12,000 men, against only 410 for the Swiss. Following the executions at Grandson the Swiss were in no mood to give any quarter to the Burgundians.

The Burgundian army never recovered from this disaster. The final battle of both the campaign and the war took place at Nancy on 5 January 1477, when a heavily outnumbered Burgundian force was crushed by an army of the duke of Lorraine, supported by a substantial force of Swiss mercenaries. Charles the Bold was killed during the battle, ending his dynasty and Burgundy's existence as a separate duchy.

Lake Murten (Lac de Morat). The Swiss advance through the Burgundian camp and down the hill pushed a section of the Burgundian Army into the lake, where they drowned.

The view from the hill of Bodemünzi (Bois de Dominque) looking down towards Murten. It was here that Charles the Bold set up his headquarters and the fortified camp known as the 'Grünhag'.

Nieuwpoort

2 July 1600

The Belgian town of Nieuwpoort has been the scene of two major battles over the centuries. The first, between a Dutch force under Maurice of Nassau and a Spanish army under Albrecht of Austria, was fought on 2 July 1600 as part of the Dutch revolt against Habsburg rule. The second, known as the battle of the Yser, was fought in October 1914 and was the culmination of the 'race to the sea' as the German and Allied armies sought to outflank one another.

The Dutch revolt had come about in response to the increasingly authoritarian and centralizing policies of Philip II, whose staunch Catholic beliefs were in direct conflict with the growing Protestant population of his Dutch provinces. Following a series of clashes the Habsburg commander, the duke of Alba, took a series of harsh measures that further alienated the population, leading to a general revolt under the leadership of William 'the Silent' of Orange. The early years of the revolt went poorly for the Dutch provinces, as the Spanish forces hemmed them in; however, the revolt survived and, following the assassination of William in 1584, the Dutch acquired an inspired military leader in William's son, Maurice of Nassau. Appointed at the age of only 20 to head the armies of the United Provinces – principally because there was no other candidate available – Maurice undertook a series of campaigns from the late 1580s onwards to consolidate and extend the Dutch republic. In 1600, the Estates General, the ruling council of the United

Provinces, ordered Maurice to take the Dutch Army into the southern Netherlands and attack the coastal town of Dunkirk, which was operating as a privateer base against Dutch trade.

The memorial to the Belgian King Albert I located beside the lock gates in Nieuwpoort. The lock gates were opened in 1914 to flood the surrounding land and to stop the German advance. The King Albert I Monument was inaugurated in 1938 on the initiative of associations of war veterans.

A statue on the promenade of Nieuwpoort is a symbol of the older, more sedate town. The title of the statue is Godin Van De Wind, meaning 'God of Wind', by Antoon Luyckx.

By 1 July Maurice had moved the majority of his 15,000-strong force across the river Yser towards Nieuwpoort, when he was confronted by a Spanish army under Archduke Albrecht of Austria. The Spanish force, roughly 9,000 strong, cut off his line of retreat and promptly destroyed his rearguard, and then advanced along the beach to attack the Dutch position. Maurice of Nassau was a great innovator in tactics and training. His men were drilled daily in both manoeuvring and the use of weaponry, so they were able to keep up a very high volume of fire on the advancing Spanish regiments. His flexibility in deploying his troops also enabled him to keep a decent reserve force of cavalry intact, which proved vital when the Spanish pushed back his centre. The repeated cavalry charges on the Spanish flanks beat them back until his infantry rallied and successfully broke the Spanish line, the first time a Dutch Army had bested the Spanish in an open battle. Casualties on both sides were high, with the Dutch losing 2,000 men and the Spanish some 2,500. Maurice was forced to withdraw and the de facto split between the northern and southern Netherlands was destined to become a formalized separation.

The mouth of the Yser with its flanking piers. The area from here to Dixmude was known as the Yser Front and was manned by the Belgian Army under King Albert during World War I.

This part of the Belgian coast, such as this stretch near Nieuwpoort-Bad, has been heavily developed with modern apartment buildings.

The dunes on the east side of the river Yser are now protected as part of the 'Natuurreservaat Ijzermonding'. In both 1600 and 1914 they provided the setting for fighting and bloodshed.

A lighthouse standing among the dunes outside of Nieuwpoort. This was the only part of Belgium to escape occupation by the Germans during World War I and the Belgian Army desperately hung onto this last toehold of their country.

The pier in Nieuwpoort-Bad was an unused part of the landscape of the war-battered western front. Piers flank the mouth of the Yser to both the right and the left.

Lützen

14 November 1632

Lützen, fought on 14 November 1632, just south-west of the city of Leipzig in Saxony, was one of the pivotal battles in the series of conflicts collectively known as the Thirty Years' War. The battle saw the deaths of the talented Imperial cavalry commander the Graf zu Pappenheim, as well as the commander of the Protestant force, the Swedish king Gustavus Adolphus.

The Thirty Years' War had been underway for 14 years prior to the battle, beginning in Bohemia as a revolt by Protestant subjects against their Catholic Habsburg monarch, Leopold II, who later became the Holy Roman Emperor. The conflict had widened into a more general German war and, following the intervention of first Denmark, then England, France and Sweden, into a northern European conflict. Sweden's entry had proved highly influential from 1630 onwards. At this point the Imperial Catholic cause had been very much in the ascendancy, but the highly trained Swedish forces under their king, Gustavus Adolphus, proved to have a genius for warfare. The Swedish force beat the Imperial forces under General Tilly at the battle of Breitenfeld in 1631, and followed this up with a further victory at the battle of Rain, where Tilly was killed, while the Swedish forces pushed on to

This stone marks the spot on the battlefield where Gustavus Adolphus is believed to have fallen, although modern research indicates the actual site may be some distance away. Already wounded, the Swedish king was being led from the battlefield when he was cut off by a force of Imperial cuirassiers, shot, run through several times by rapiers before being shot in the head as a coup de grace.

Munich. This led to the appointment of Albrecht von Wallenstein as commander of the Imperial forces, who in short order drove the Saxons out of Bohemia and moved to Nuremberg, where he drove off an attempt by Gustavus Adolphus to storm his position in September 1632. Following this setback the Swedes moved south into

Bavaria, while Wallenstein moved north-eastwards to campaign against Saxony, with Leipzig as his main target. Realizing that the Imperial forces would block his communications with Sweden, as well as threatening one of his allies, Gustavus Adolphus marched northwards, reaching Erfurt by 7 November 1632. On 14 November Wallenstein split his forces and retreated towards Leipzig, not expecting any further Swedish action that year. However, Gustavus Adolphus followed him and Wallenstein, having summoned back his detached force under Pappenheim, positioned his army around the village of Lützen.

The battle started with Gustavus Adolphus leading his cavalry of the Swedish right wing against the Imperial left. They broke through the Imperial cavalry here but were counterattacked by Pappenheim's returning cavalry in an action that led to Pappenheim's death. The fighting in this area of the battlefield also cost Gustavus Adolphus his life, as he was injured, cut off and killed by a group of Imperial cuirassiers (heavily armoured cavalry). In the centre of the battlefield the advancing Swedish infantry were pinned in place by Imperial infantry before being cut down by cavalry from the flanks and retiring in disorder. A Swedish attack on the Imperial right, though initially successful, was also driven off.

In the mid-afternoon the Swedes were rallied by their new commander, Bernhard of Sachsen-Weimar, and attacked once more, driving the Imperial line back and ending the fighting for the day. During the night Wallenstein withdrew, abandoning his artillery on the field, and retreating to Leipzig.

The battlefield and village of Lützen hold many memorials to the hero of the Protestant cause, Gustavus Adolphus – the Lion of the North. This statue of the Swedish king stands outside the city hall.

The battle was fought around the Leipzig to Lützen road, which still exists though it is considerably wider and faster, particularly since the reunification of Germany in 1990.

Fehrbellin

28 June 1675

The battle of Fehrbellin, fought on 28 June 1675, was a conclusive Swedish defeat at the hands of Brandenburg-Prussia. Although the long-term strategic effects of the battle were limited, it served to reduce Sweden's reputation as a great military power and heralded the rise of Brandenburg-Prussia as a military power in the region. It also boosted the reputation of both the Great Elector, Frederick William, and the house of Hohenzollern.

The battle came about as part of the Dutch War instigated by France's King Louis XIV in 1672. Having successfully defeated a coalition of his enemies in the War of Devolution, Louis XIV entered into an alliance with Charles II of England to attack the Dutch United Provinces both by land and sea. Sweden was also persuaded to join this coalition. The initial land campaign went well for the French, with Nijmegen falling on 9 July 1672, but the Dutch rallied, appointing William of Orange (later William III of England) as their head of state and flooded the approaches to Amsterdam to protect the city. Dutch naval victories against the English, notably at Texel in August 1673, also caused England to withdraw from what was an unpopular war at home, while France's early success had provoked the Holy Roman Emperor, the king of Spain and elector of Brandenburg-Prussia to enter the war on the side of the Dutch in 1673 and 1674. The Brandenburg-Prussian forces were defeated by the French under their great commander Turenne at the battle of Turkheim in Alsace on

5 January 1675, forcing the German troops back. In order to remove them altogether from the conflict, Louis XIV persuaded his Swedish allies to invade Brandenburg-Prussia while the main army was absent.

A force of 13,000 men under Count Waldemar von Wrangel invaded from the Swedish possession of Pomerania, taking control of much of Brandenburg-Prussia. On hearing of this development, Frederick William ordered a scorched-earth policy to deny the Swedes supplies and, withdrawing his forces from the coalition against France, marched the 250km (155 miles) back to Brandenburg-Prussia in only a fortnight. The Swedes had been compelled to split their forces in order to obtain supplies and, realizing this, Frederick William moved to split the two sections of the Swedish Army by occupying the town of Rathenow. His army, under its commander Georg von Derfflinger, managed to take the town, and in response the Swedes attempted to reunite their army around the town of Fehrbellin. However, they found the bridge across the river destroyed and were trapped until it could be repaired. Meanwhile the Brandenburg-Prussian forces took up a strong position on heights opposite them. The Brandenburg-Prussians used their artillery well, causing heavy casualties on the Swedish right flank, before attacking it with cavalry. The Swedes managed to hang on until the bridge was repaired and successfully withdrew their army across it, thus ending the battle. Casualties on both sides were roughly equal, with about 500 losses, but Frederick William remained in control of the field and claimed victory. The Swedish defeat also provoked Denmark into invading Swedish territory, thus starting the Scanian War.

A memorial to the battle of Fehrbellin erected at Hakenberg in 1800. The memorial is supposed to mark the point where the Brandenburg Dragoons under the duke of Homburg broke through the Swedish right flank.

A column was erected in 1879 to celebrate the battle. It stands on the position occupied by the Brandenburg-Prussian artillery, which was to prove so influential during the battle.

A tree-lined alley crossing the battlefield of Fehrbellin going from Hakenberg to the south. These alleys are a typical feature of the scenery throughout the state of Brandenburg and, in general, are more common in the regions of the former East Germany.

Vienna

12 September 1683

The siege of Vienna and battle of Kahlenberg that ended it proved to be the furthest point reached by the Ottoman Empire in their sequence of conquests in south-east Europe. Following the Imperial victory in the battle, the Ottoman conquests were rolled back one by one throughout the late 17th and 18th centuries. Prior to the siege there had been a period of peace between the Holy Roman and Ottoman empires that had lasted from 1664, and was due to expire in 1684. However, following the promptings of his Grand Vizier, Kara Mustafa, Sultan Mehmed IV decided in 1682 to repudiate the treaty and launch a military campaign against the Holy Roman Empire with aim of taking its capital, Vienna. Leopold I, the Holy Roman Emperor, was already faced with an uprising by Imre Thököly in the lands he controlled in Hungary, while Louis XIV of France was looking to take control of Habsburg possessions in the west. He was therefore unprepared for war with a resurgent Ottoman Empire.

Following the decision to invade, the Ottoman Army first moved from Istanbul to Adrianople, where they remained for four months before moving on to Belgrade, where the Sultan remained while Kara Mustafa led the army on to surround Vienna and, having taken the city of Györ on the way, arrived before Vienna on 14 July. The Ottoman force was divided into two, with the force tasked with besieging the city numbering around 15,000, and another army of around 70,000 men covering the siege and raiding the surrounding countryside.

When Leopold I realized the level of the Ottoman threat he assembled the Imperial Army of 37,000 men under Charles Sixte of Lorraine. This force mounted a series of delaying actions in front of the Ottoman advance before withdrawing

The city of Vienna seen from the top of the Kahlenberg. In 1683 the outer suburbs were destroyed by the defenders to provide clear fields of fire and to deny them to the Turks.

A view of the Leopoldsberg and Kahlenberg from the Danube as it runs through the city centre. The Ottoman main camp was located between the city and the hills in the background.

St Leopold's Church on top of the Leopoldsberg. The Leopoldsberg, originally known as the Kahlenberg, was the location of the battle that saved Vienna on 12 September 1683.

northwards, leaving a garrison of around 12,000 men under Count Ernst Rüdiger von Starhemberg in defence of Vienna. The Austrians destroyed the outer suburbs of Vienna to create clear fields of fire and awaited the Ottoman assault, which was not long in coming. The Ottomans set up siege batteries surrounding the city and began the construction of a series of trenches approaching the city fortifications. Over the next two months the Ottomans pressed forwards, digging a series of mines beneath the Austrian fortifications as they strove to break through into the city. The Austrian position became more and more desperate as their numbers dwindled until, on 8 September, there were only 4,000 able-bodied men left. However, a relieving army now arrived, consisting of a Holy League of Imperial, Bavarian and German troops, as well as 20,000 Polish troops under John III Sobieski, king of Poland, who commanded the army. This force assembled on the Kahlenberg outside Vienna and the Ottomans formed up to face them. On 12 September battle commenced, with Saxon and Imperial troops launching an attack on the Ottoman right wing. The Ottomans then carried out a general assault on the Holy League line, which was pushed back, before a Polish cavalry charge shattered the Ottoman right wing in the late afternoon. With both flanks defeated, Kara Mustafa withdrew, abandoning the siege and eventually falling back to Belgrade, where he was executed on 25 September on the Sultan's orders.

The southern slope of the Kahlenberg looking towards the city centre of Vienna. This may well have been where the Ottoman first position was situated on 12 September 1683. The Polish winged hussars poured down this slope to break the Ottoman lines and seal the victory for the Holy League forces.

Blenheim

13 August 1704

Although the War of the Spanish Succession carried on for nine years after the battle of Blenheim, which took place on 13 August 1704, it is possible to argue that it was the war's most significant encounter. It prevented the French troops of Louis XIV from knocking the Holy Roman Empire out of the war, thus shattering the Grand Alliance that had developed as a bulwark against French ambitions.

The root cause of the conflict was the accession to the Spanish throne of Louis XIV's grandson, Philip of Anjou, in 1700. Louis took this as an opportunity to occupy fortresses in the Spanish Netherlands, an act that threatened the Dutch. At the same time conflict broke out in Italy with the Austrians, whose royal family had a valid claim to the Spanish throne as well. The English entered the conflict on the side of the Dutch and Austrians, forming the Grand Alliance with Denmark, Prussia, Hanover and a number of other German states, as they felt threatened by France's increasing dominance over Europe. War broke out in 1702 and an English expeditionary force was sent to support the Dutch under the command of John Churchill, Duke of Marlborough. Although he won some successes in Flanders in 1703, the situation for Austria was bleak as a revolt had broken out in Hungary while Bavaria had sided with the French, and a French army under Marshal Villars headed for Bavaria ready for a campaign to take Vienna in 1704.

Marlborough resolved to move his army to the Danube to link up with Prince Eugene of Savoy's Austrian forces and defend Vienna. He pretended that he intended to fight a campaign along the Moselle, deceiving both the French and his Dutch allies, and marched his army down the Rhine, shadowed by a French army under Marshal Villeroi all the way. Passing the Moselle at Koblenz, he pushed on towards Donauwörth on the Danube where he linked up with Prince Eugene and

The village of Blindheim in Bavaria, known as Blenheim in English, and the location after which the battle is named. It is also known as the battle of Höchstädt after the larger town to the south.

launched an attack on the strong fortification of the Schellenberg, capturing it in a *coup de main* on 2 July 1704. Another French army under Marshal Tallard managed to break through to support the Bavarian forces under the Elector and the main French Army under Marsin, who had replaced Villars in the winter, and the Franco-Bavarian force crossed the Danube to threaten Marlborough's supply lines, making camp near the village of Blenheim. Marlborough and Eugene advanced to meet them and committed to battle on 13 August. Marlborough attacked the flank of Tallard's army, based at the village of Blenheim itself, while Eugene attacked the combined Franco-Bavarian force under the Elector and Marsin. Although Eugene's attacks were unsuccessful, both flanking attacks sucked in the French and Bavarian reserves, leaving Tallard with no help when Marlborough launched his uncommitted cavalry at the French centre late in the day. They destroyed or captured the French infantry in the centre and drove the cavalry off, with many of them drowning in the Danube, leaving Marlborough's infantry free to encircle and finish off the French troops trapped in Blenheim itself. The Elector and Marsin withdrew in reasonably good order and Vienna had been saved.

An observation tower gives a fine view over the battlefield. Here it looks towards Unterglauheim. The tower is located mid-way between Blenheim and Unterglauheim, on the spot where Marlborough's cavalry broke through the French line at around 4pm.

A memorial stone in Unterglauheim records the events of the day, stating that the village was destroyed by fire at 8am before being attacked by Marlborough's cavalry at 4pm the same day.

Flowers in a field near Höchstädt. The French casualties in the battle were enormous, with 20,000 killed, drowned or wounded, and 14,190 captured, including Marshal Tallard himself and 40 generals.

The battlefield between the villages of Lutzingen and Oberglauheim towards the river Nebel. This was the section of the battlefield occupied by the Franco-Bavarian forces under the Elector and Marisn. Prince Eugene of Savoy repeatedly attacked here, preventing them from going to the assistance of Marshal Tallard.

Gadebusch

9 December 1712

The battle of Gadebusch, fought on 9 December 1712 in what is now northern Germany, was the last significant Swedish victory of what is known as the Great Northern War. Swedish involvement in the Thirty Years' War had brought it a substantial empire throughout northern Europe, turning the Baltic into a Swedish lake, with most of the Baltic states and part of northern Germany under her control. This alienated her neighbours, particularly Russia which was undergoing a period of modernization under the rule of Peter the Great. With the death of Charles XI of Sweden in 1697, his 14-year-old son Charles XII ascended the throne and Sweden's neighbours saw an opportunity to dismember the Swedish Empire. Russia, Denmark-Norway and Poland-Saxony entered into an alliance and declared war in March 1700. The young Swedish king won a number of striking victories in the first years of the war, knocking Denmark-Norway out of the alliance in August 1700, destroying a Russian Army at Narva in November 1700 and reducing Poland-Saxony by 1706. However, a campaign deep into Russia came to grief at the battle of Poltava in 1709, and Charles XII spent the next five years in exile. With their king trapped in Turkey, a council now governed Sweden. Russia, Denmark-Norway and Poland-Saxony entered into an alliance once more and began to reduce Sweden's territories around the southern shore of the Baltic, as well as in Scania. By 1712, all of Sweden's major possessions had been lost apart from forts scattered around the Baltic. A Swedish Army under Count Magnus Gustafsson Stenbock with an army of around 14,000 men protected the strategically important port of Stralsund, which was threatened by a joint Russian-Saxon army, while a Danish army was positioned around Hamburg.

Unable to launch an attack on the Russians, Stenbock moved his army westward to confront the Danes, who were now located near the village of Gadebusch. Although the Russians were unable to commit their infantry to help their ally, they did dispatch 3,500 Saxon cavalry under Jacob Heinrich von Flemming. After a period of manoeuvering the two sides met in a frontal battle on the morning of 9 December 1712. The Danes, with around 16,000 men, together with the 3,500 Saxons, outnumbered the 14,000 Swedes, but the Swedes had significantly more artillery, which was to prove decisive in the end.

Following two hours of sustained artillery fire, the Swedes advanced in the centre whilst their cavalry launched an attack on the Danish cavalry to the left, pushing them back. The Saxon cavalry was unable to break the Swedish left, despite repeated attacks, and the Danish-Saxon line was pushed back all along the front. By the end of the day the Danes and Saxons were forced to withdraw from the battlefield, leaving behind all their artillery, and having suffered over 3,500 casualties compared to only 1,500 for the Swedes. The victory earned Stenbock a promotion to field marshal, but had little long-term strategic effect as within six months, in May 1713, his forces were defeated and he surrendered after a battle at Tonning.

Swedish and Danish flags throughout the landscape show the position of the various forces involved in the battle. Gadebusch proved to be the last major Swedish success in the region and the beginning of the end for Sweden as a major European power.

This image shows the central section of the battlefield, with the starting positions of the Swedish troops located in the middle of the image. From here they advanced to push back the Danish line at about 1pm on 9 December 1712.

Leuthen

5 December 1757

The battle of Leuthen was one of a pair of battles, fought late in 1757, which rescued Frederick the Great from a perilous position in the Seven Years' War and enabled him to fight on into 1758.

Prussia had captured the rich province of Silesia during the War of the Austrian Succession in 1740–48 and, despite his possession of the region being confirmed by a number of treaties, Frederick the Great became convinced that Austria was assembling a coalition to take it back. He launched a pre-emptive strike on Saxony in August 1756, thus precipitating the Seven Years' War in Europe. Frederick successfully conquered Saxony, driving the elector and his court into exile in Poland, before invading Bohemia in 1757. Despite a hard-fought victory at Prague, he was beaten at the battle of Kolin while the Russians defeated a Prussian army at Gross Jägersdorf in East Prussia.

Frederick's position was difficult, but he first defeated a joint French and Imperial army at the battle of Rossbach on 5 November 1757 before turning his attention to the Austrian Army that had invaded Silesia.

This Austrian Army was around 80,000 strong and under the command of Prince Charles of Lorraine, though the victor of Kolin, Graf von Daun, continued to run the army on a day-to-day basis. When Frederick had moved west to fight the Franco-Imperial force, this Austrian Army moved into Silesia and defeated a Prussian force at the battle of Breslau on 22 November, capturing

the city itself on 24 November. After his victory at Rossbach, Frederick marched east once more to confront the Austrians, and, having gathered the defeated remnants of the Prussian Army based in Breslau, he arrived in Parchwitz on 28 November having marched 290km (180 miles) in 15 days. On 4 December

The churchyard today. In 1757 it was defended by the Infanterie Regiment Rot-Würzburg, which fought valiantly until overwhelmed by superior Prussian numbers just after 4pm.

Following the end of World War II German Silesia, fought over for so many years, became part of modern-day Poland and many aspects of the previously German region changed, especially the names of the villages. So Leuthen became Lutynia, Schriegwitz became Jarzabkowice and Sagschütz became Zakrzyce.

A major part of the battle took place in the village of Leuthen itself, with intense fighting taking place on the streets and in the houses. The churchyard, located above much of the rest of the village and possessing stout walls, became a centre of Austrian resistance.

he marched his 35,000-strong force out to attack the Austrians, who had come out of Breslau and were now around the town of Leuthen.

The Austrians had drawn up their forces into a 9km-long line (5½ miles) in order to try to prevent Frederick from turning their flanks; they also kept a mobile reserve behind the main line. Frederick resolved to attack the Austrian left, while deceiving the Austrians into thinking he would attack in the centre. His plan worked perfectly, and Prince Charles of Lorraine moved the Austrian reserve to the north of the battlefield while Frederick's troops marched south and wheeled so they were in a position to roll up the Austrian line from south to north. The Austrians struggled to realign their troops and, despite a desperate cavalry counter-attack, the Prussians rolled up the Austrian position, breaking through the line and capturing the village of Leuthen, before Frederick's cavalry broke through the Austrian cavalry and pushed them back onto their own infantry, which finished off the Austrians who broke and ran. The battle ended with the Austrians losing 7,000 men as casualties and 22,000 as prisoners of war. The Prussians suffered some 6,400 casualties, and followed up the victory to retake Breslau and drive the Austrians out of Silesia.

The landscape between Leuthen and Sagschütz at the Schriegwitz junction, where the Prussian infantry rolled up the Austrian line on the afternoon of 5 December 1757. The newly constructed buildings are part of Leuthen's southern suburbs..

The battlefield of Leuthen is located 25km (16 miles) east of Wroclaw in modern-day Poland, formerly known as Breslau. Shown here are the flat fields between Sagschütz (now Zakrzyce) and Gohlau (now Galow) where Frederick's army began its assault on the left wing of the Austrian force.

Valmy

20 September 1792

The battle of Valmy was the decisive engagement in the first year of the French Revolutionary Wars that stretched from 1792 to 1802. Ever since the start of the Revolution in 1789, the crowned heads of Europe had looked unfavourably on the situation in France, and in April 1791 Russia, Prussia and Austria had issued the Declaration of Pillnitz, which threatened France with military action should any harm come to Louis XVI and his family. Following this, and other developments such as the attempted flight by Louis to the Austrian Netherlands, France declared war on Austria on 20 April 1792. A revolutionary army under the French Foreign Minister Dumouriez immediately attempted an invasion of the Austrian Netherlands, but with little success as the disorganized French troops broke under fire — even murdering their own officers on one occasion. This encouraged Prussia to enter the conflict alongside Austria and an army was assembled near Koblenz to invade France, take Paris and restore Louis XVI to his position on the throne. This army, commanded by the duke of Brunswick, was a mixture of Prussians, Austrians, Hessians and French émigré troops, and it crossed the French border on 19 August 1792, heading for the border fortress of Longwy. It duly fell on 23 August, and was followed by Verdun on 2 September before the army turned towards Paris. However, the French had reorganized their forces after the disappointments of the Austrian Netherlands and now had two armies to face the Prussians: the Army of the North under Dumouriez and the Army of the Centre under Kellermann.

The view towards the village of Valmy, situated to the rear of Kellermann's Army of the Centre.

Guns positioned at the Kellermann memorial. These guns are not the original ones used during the battle but captured British ones. The ability of the French artillery at Valmy proved decisive.

Dumouriez moved at once to block the duke of Brunswick's army as it moved through the Argonne Forest, summoning Kellermann from Metz to join him. However, before the Army of the Centre had time to arrive, the Prussian Army had managed to get around the French force and now stood between them and Paris. However, the duke of Brunswick was unwilling to leave such a large hostile force to his rear and so committed to battle on 20 September 1792.

By this stage Kellermann's Army of the Centre had arrived and taken up position in front of Dumouriez's forces at the village of Valmy. This gave the French some 52,000 men compared to the Prussians' 34,000. The French positions came under artillery attack in the morning of the 20th, but they held

firm against all expectations and when the Prussian columns advanced, the French artillery drove them back with accurate fire. The duke of Brunswick did not press home his attacks and retired from the field, pulling back towards the Rhine. Throughout the course of the battle the French suffered some 300 casualties and the Prussians 180, but Paris had been saved. The following day saw the abolition of the French monarchy and the establishment of the First Republic, while the execution of Louis XVI in January 1793 saw Spain and Great Britain join the First Coalition against France, setting the stage for the years of war that followed.

The windmill near the Kellermann memorial. This is not the original one from the time of the battle but a replacement, built in 2005 following the destruction of the previous windmill in a storm in 1999.

A view of the battlefield from Valmy Hill. The village of Valmy is seen to the left. The windmill to the right is where the centre of the French Army was based on 20 September 1792.

The Kellermann Memorial, constructed in 1892, 100 years after the battle, depicts the general brandishing his hat and sabre. Kellermann was later granted the title Duke of Valmy by Napoleon, and requested that when he died his heart be buried on the battlefield.

⊹ Austerlitz

2 December 1805

Fought on 2 December 1805 near what is now the Czech town of Slavkov u Brna, the battle of Austerlitz is rightly seen as one of Napoleon Bonaparte's defining victories, a battle that changed the face of Europe and caused the final collapse of the Holy Roman Empire. The French *Grande Armée* decisively defeated a combined Austrian and Russian force and broke apart the Third Coalition so painstakingly assembled by the British Prime Minister, William Pitt.

This coalition had its origins in an Anglo-Swedish agreement of December 1804, with the Russians signing an alliance with Great Britain in April 1805 and Austria joining in a few months later. The Third Coalition, as it became known, drew up plans for a series of combined offensives through Hanover, Bavaria and Northern Italy before pushing into France itself. Napoleon, having learned of the Allied plans, moved his army from its main encampment outside Boulogne, where he had been planning an invasion of England, and turned his forces eastwards to confront this new threat.

The first major act of the campaign was the French encirclement of the Austrian forces under General Mack, who had advanced into Bavaria with 72,000 men and occupied the city of Ulm, where he awaited the advance of the

Russians under General Kutusov. Having despatched a force of 40,000 men under Murat to hold the Austrians in place, Napoleon led the 210,000 men of his *Grande Armée* across the Rhine north of Ulm on 24/25 September, reaching the Danube on 2 October and captured Augsburg. They were now free to

A concrete factory in Holubice, which is located where the Allied right wing fought on 2 December 1805. Much of the equipment in the factory is painted or decorated in a way that highlights the heritage of the site as one of the most important battlefields of the Napoleonic Wars.

A view of the peace memorial on the Pratzeberg. Although situated on property owned by the French Government, the memorial is dedicated to all the participants, with three corners representing each of the major powers involved and the fourth the Czech participants. The centre of the monument contains an ossuary holding the bones of those who died in the battle.

encircle the main Austrian army, which surrendered on 20 October. Napoleon now pushed on to meet the advancing Russians under Kutusov, who realized his army's weakness and retreated ahead of the French, fighting a series of delaying actions before withdrawing north of the Austrian capital, Vienna, which fell to the French on 15 November. Here Kutusov joined another Russian army under Buxhöwden and the Tsar, giving him a combined force of some 90,000 men while Napoleon halted his force of 53,000 at Brünn to rest and reorganize.

Napoleon resolved to lure the combined Russo-Austrian force into a battleground of his own choosing and retreated back to Austerlitz, deliberately weakening his right flank to encourage the Allies to attack there. At the same time he summoned his two detached corps from Iglau and Vienna, which increased the number of men at his disposal to 75,000. The Allied commanders took the bait and, on the morning of 2 December, launched a major attack under Bagration on the French right wing under Soult. Major fighting took place around the villages of Sokolnitz and Telnitz, which changed hands a number of times over the course of the day, before the arrival of fresh French troops under Davout stabilized the line, provoking the Allies to weaken their centre to assist the attack on the French right. This was the moment when Napoleon launched his major assault on the Allied centre on the Pratzen Heights, while at the same time two French corps advanced on the Allied right to prevent them from intervening in the centre. The French attack on the Pratzen Heights succeeded, splitting the Allied army in two and, despite a major counterattack at Pratzen by the Russian Imperial Guard, the French held on and, reinforced by their own guard, drove through the Allied lines and annihilated Büxhowden's forces on the Allied left. Over the course of the battle the Allies lost 25,000 men compared to only 8,500 for the French. The Austrians signed an armistice on the 4th while the Russians withdrew homewards.

The memorial on top of the Pratzeberg, the highest point on the Pratzen Heights and the battlefield as a whole. This peace memorial was built in 1910–12 and is dedicated to all who fought in the battle.

The Žuráň Hill at Austerlitz. This hill was the site of Napoleon's headquarters and the Imperial Guard at the beginning of the battle before he moved forwards onto the Pratzen Heights. It was from here that the major attack on the Allied centre was launched. The trees on the top of the hill are part of a memorial built in 1930.

The centre of the battlefield at Austerlitz is dominated by the Pratzen Heights, the key tactical feature on the battlefield which was seized by the French in their major assault in the morning, before being counterattacked by the Russian Imperial guard under Kutusov. This view shows the ridge between the Pratzen and Vinohrady hills.

Jena and Auerstedt

14 October 1806

Following his crushing victory at Austerlitz in 1805, Napoleon had knocked Austria out of the war but Russia still remained an active enemy. Prussia had remained neutral during the campaign of 1805, though it had come perilously close to joining the forces of the Fourth Coalition against Napoleon. In the end, following his victory, Napoleon was able to extract a treaty from Prussia that compelled her to declare war on Great Britain as well as surrender territory to the French; in return Prussia would receive the British territory of Hanover. However, the formation of the Confederation of the Rhine in July 1806 left Prussia isolated and Napoleon's offer to the British of the return of Hanover in exchange for a general peace left her betrayed. The war party in the Prussian Government won control, leading to a Prussian agreement with Russia in August and the decision to go to war.

Napoleon did not receive news of this decision until September, when he began to mobilize his forces and assemble them in southern Germany. The Prussians issued an ultimatum to Napoleon, giving him until 8 October to respond. On the 8th he crossed over into Prussian territory with three columns, each consisting of two corps. The first encounters at Schleiz and Saalfeld went the way of the French, with the latter action causing the death of Prince Louis of Prussia, and Napoleon pushed on, capturing the towns of Jena and Gera. On the 13th the French V Corps under Marshal Lannes encountered 40,000 Prussians under Prince Hohenlohe just outside of Jena. Lannes reported this to Napoleon as the Prussian main army, and prepared for battle. Napoleon at once began to

The Krippendorf Windmill formed part of the Prussian line before the battle, but was taken by the French on their way to victory.

draw up the four corps with him while also summoning the two corps under Davout and Bernadotte that were located to the north at Zeitz and Naumburg.

On the morning of the 14th the four French corps at Jena advanced on the Prussian forces who, instead of retreating towards the main body of their army,

One of the 'tactical memorial stones' that are scattered across the battlefield of Jena. Those dealing with French troops have a round top, while the Prussian ones are peaked.

launched a counter-attack against the superior French. Despite an impetuous attack by Marshal Ney's VI Corps that came close to opening a gap in the French centre when it was driven back, the numerical superiority of the French kept up a constant pressure on the Prussian line. Despite the arrival of reinforcements under Ruchel, the Prussians eventually broke, having lost over 20,000 men for only 6,000 French casualties.

Meanwhile, marching from Naumburg, Davout's III Corps of 27,000 men ran directly into the main Prussian force of 50,000 men under the duke of Brunswick at Auerstedt. The French force managed to beat off repeated cavalry attacks by the Prussians under Blücher. A general Prussian advance almost managed to turn the French position, but the loss of several senior commanders to French fire, including the duke of Brunswick, left the Prussian Army leaderless and unable to launch coordinated attacks. This allowed the French to regroup and take the attack to the Prussians, pushing them off the battlefield in disorder. Davout had managed to defeat an army twice the size of his force.

Details of information, such as times, are shown on the 'tactical memorial stones'.

The battlefield of Jena between the villages of Vierzehnheiligen and the Krippendorf Windmill. Visible is a 'tactical memorial stone' marking the position of particular groups of troops and giving their movements and strengths.

The battlefield of Auerstedt near Hassenhausen. The trees are part of the memorial to the duke of Brunswick who was mortally wounded at the battle. He died later in November 1806.

Leipzig

16–19 October 1813

The Russian campaign of 1812 had proved disastrous for Napoleon. His *Grande Armée* had been destroyed in the retreat from Moscow, causing his unwilling Prussian and Austrian allies to desert the French cause. The Prussian General Von Yorck signed the Convention of Tauroggen with the Russians on 30 December 1812, taking his corps over to their side, while the Austrian troops under the Prince Von Schwarzenburg declared neutrality and retreated back to Austria. On 28 February 1813 Prussia formally joined forces with Russia in the Treaty of Kalisch, declaring war once more on France on 16 March 1813, while the Austrians declared war on 12 August 1813, setting the stage for a climactic campaign in Germany and France.

Napoleon had returned to Paris ahead of the remnants of his *Grande Armée*, which finally straggled into East Prussia with only 100,000 men remaining of the 650,000 that had advanced into Russia. Through a feverish process of combing out existing units, calling up the class of 1813, assimilating National Guardsmen into the regular army, recruiting marines and sailors from the blockaded French fleet and withdrawing troops from Spain, Napoleon managed to assemble another *Grande Armée*, consisting of some 400,000 men, with which to confront the threat posed by the Sixth Coalition.

The Russian Army under Kutusov moved west and, having joined with Prussian forces, the army, now commanded by Wittgenstein due to Kutusov's

illness, met the French at the battle of Lützen on 2 May, which, along with the battle of Bautzen on 20–21 May, were French victories, though hard-fought ones. These battles led to an armistice between the two sides, which was extended into August when the Austrians and Swedes joined the Sixth Coalition.

The Völkerschlachtdenkmal, a memorial to the 'Battle of Nations' built to commemorate the centenary of the Allied victory. The monument, which stands to the south of Leipzig, is over 90m (295ft) high.

Many of the famous sections of the Leipzig battlefield are now covered by urban development, such as this autobahn located near Güldengossa, from where the Prussian and Russian guards advanced to counter a French offensive on the morning of 16 October 1813.

The Allied forces were now organized into four main armies: the Army of Silesia under Blücher (95,000), the Army of the North under the former French marshal Bernadotte (110,000), the Army of Bohemia under Schwarzenburg (230,000) and the Army of Poland under Bennigsen (60,000), of which Schwarzenburg was the supreme commander.

St Alexij Gedächtniskirche in Leipzig. This Russian Orthodox Church was built to commemorate the 22,000 Russian soldiers who fell during the battle of Leipzig.

Napoleon meanwhile split his army into two, keeping 250,000 men with him and detaching 120,000 to attack Berlin under Oudinot. The assault on Berlin failed and, having won a victory at Dresden but having seen three of his corps defeated in separate encounters, Napoleon retreated to Leipzig to protect his supply lines. Here, between 16 and 19 October 1813, the largest battle seen in Europe prior to World War I would be fought. The forces of the Sixth Coalition, numbering some 330,000 men under Schwarzenburg and Blücher, assaulted the French, who had some 190,000 under Napoleon. The first two days of the battle saw a number of shifts in fortune as the Allies tried to break the French lines with little success. However, the arrival of Bernadotte and his men on the evening of the 17th meant that the French were heavily pressed on the 18th and forced back onto Leipzig itself. This, combined with the defection of his Saxon contingent, led Napoleon to order a retreat on the night of 18/19 October. The premature demolition of a bridge across the river Elster left half the *Grande Armée* trapped in Leipzig, where they were either captured or killed, confirming the battle as a significant defeat for Napoleon. The war would now move into France itself.

A detail of the crypt inside the Völkerschlachtdenkmal. Casualty figures for the battle are uncertain, with estimates ranging from 80,000 to 110,000 killed and wounded on all sides. The French suffered the most, losing 38,000 as casualties and as many as 50,000 as prisoners of war.

A memorial located between Wachau and Güldengossa on the southern part of the battlefield. Located in the former East Germany, this joint Prussian and Russian memorial was built in 1988, before the collapse of the Eastern Bloc. It marks the position from where the Russian troops started their attack against Wachau on 16 October, with the city of Leipzig visible in the background.

Waterloo

18 June 1815

The battle of Waterloo was the culminating encounter of the Napoleonic Wars that had been fought throughout Europe and the world from 1803 onwards. An Anglo-Dutch force under the duke of Wellington and a Prussian army under Marshal Blücher decisively defeated the *Grande Armée* under Napoleon Bonaparte, leaving the Bonapartist cause finished and Napoleon himself exiled to the Atlantic island of St Helena. It was truly a battle that changed the face of modern Europe.

On 26 February Napoleon escaped from exile on the island of Elba and landed in the south of France. Assembling an army of his old soldiers around him he moved slowly towards Paris, gathering support on the way, and taking control of the French state once more. Immediately a Seventh Coalition against him was organized by the countries attending the Congress of Vienna, and the duke of Wellington was put in charge of an Anglo-Dutch army of 90,000 men that was assembled to the north-east of France. In addition to this, a Prussian army of 120,000 men under Marshal Blücher also moved to Belgium. In the face of this threat Napoleon acted decisively, moving across the Sambre on 15 June with an army of 125,000, the vast majority of whom were veterans of his earlier campaigns, divided into three: Marshal Ney with the left wing, Napoleon with the reserve and Marshal Grouchy with the right wing. On 16 June he attacked Blücher's Prussians at Ligny with the reserve and right wing, driving them defeated

from the battlefield. The Prussians retreated northwards to Wavre, pursued by the French right wing under Grouchy. Wellington, facing Ney at Quatre Bras, was forced back and withdrew to the ridge of Mont St Jean, near the village of

The Butte de Lion dominates the battlefield at Waterloo. Constructed by William I of the Netherlands, it was built as a monument to his son, the prince of Orange, who commanded the combined Dutch and Belgian troops at the battle.

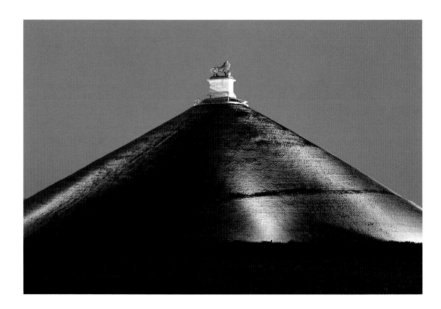

Very soon after the battle the site became the centre of a burgeoning tourist industry and, arguably, the first theme park in Europe. Part of this development is the Napoleon Shop and Wax Museum at the bottom of the Butte de Lion.

By this point in the afternoon the presence of the Prussians on the battlefield was making itself felt, as they began to pressurise the French right around Plancenoit. Realizing that this was his last opportunity for victory, Napoleon committed the Imperial Guard in an attack on the Allied line. In an epic encounter with the British Foot Guards, the French guardsmen were driven back, leading to a general advance by the Allied Army. This, combined with the Prussian assault from the right, ensured an Allied victory and the French were driven from the battlefield.

Early morning fog on the battlefield of Waterloo. This image shows the view from the position occupied by Bylandt's Brigade of the 2nd Dutch-Belgian Division, which was exposed in front of the main Allied line and shattered by French artillery fire before it broke and ran.

Created in 1912 by Louis Dumoulin in celebration of the 100th anniversary of the battle, the Panorama of Waterloo is a 360-degree painting depicting the major events of the battle. It is an impressive 110m (360ft) in circumference and 12m (40ft) high.

Waterloo, where he deployed his army. Having heard from Blücher that he was able and willing to reinforce the Allied position, Wellington resolved to fight.

The battle started on the morning of 18 June with a French attack on the fortified farm of Hougoumont on the Allied right and, despite fierce fighting throughout the day, this position remained in British hands. Next, a major attack was launched against the Allied centre at 1.30pm, supported by a grand battery of massed French artillery. This assault came close to breaking the Allied lines in the centre, but a charge by heavy brigades of British cavalry managed to halt the French infantry and push them back, though at great cost. At 4pm Marshal Ney launched another assault on the British centre using the massed French cavalry, which was forced to withdraw after suffering heavy loses. However, late in the afternoon the fortified farm La Haye Sainte on the British left was captured by the French, opening up the British centre once more.

The view from the centre of the British line, the position occupied by the prince of Orange and Maitland's Brigade of Foot Guards looking across to the Belle Alliance, which was Napoleon's headquarters for much of the battle.

The Butte de Lion (Lion's Mound), erected between 1824 and 1826 on the spot where the Prince of Orange was wounded in the shoulder by a musket ball. The mound stands 40m (130ft) above the battlefield and the lion on top looks towards France.

Solferino

24 June 1859

Solferino proved to be the conclusive battle of the Second Italian War of Independence and led to the formation of the independent state of Italy under King Victor Emmanuel II, the former king of Piedmont-Sardinia. The battle, fought on 24 June 1859, also proved to be the largest encounter since the battle of Leipzig during the Napoleonic Wars, and it would be the last time that three heads of state took to the field of battle in command of their respective forces: the French emperor, Napoleon III, the Piedmontese-Sardinian King, Victor Emmanuel II and the Austrian emperor, Franz Josef.

The campaign started in late April 1859 when the Sardinians, bolstered by French promises of aid in case of war, rejected Austrian demands to disarm and withdraw from the frontiers. Immediately French troops began to move into Piedmont by rail and by sea and, although the Austrian Army of Lombardy under General Gyulai crossed the river Ticino into Piedmontese territory, Gyulai's indecisive leadership ensured that they did not prosper and withdrew in the face of a growing French presence in early May. The French and Sardinians decided to take the war into Austrian territory and advanced on

The memorial to the Red Cross located at Solferino. The founder of the Red Cross, Henri Dunant, was present at the battle and was so horrified by the conditions and the slaughter that he convened the 1863 Geneva Conference that led directly to the foundation of the International Red Cross and the Geneva Convention in 1864.

Milan. Following engagements at Montebello on 20 May and Palestro on 30/31 May, the first major battle of the campaign occurred at Magenta on 4 June. Here, in a confused and bloody encounter, the Austrians were forced out of the town and Gyulai decided to withdraw to a series of fortresses to the

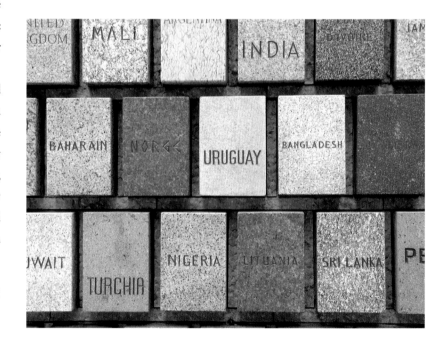

Fields near the village of Rebecco, 7.5km south of Solferino. Heavy fighting was seen here in the defence of Guidizzolo, which is 3km away.

superiority in terms of equipment and training, and this was to prove decisive in what became a true soldiers' battle. Following the initial skirmishes the French concentrated their forces in the centre and, following hard fighting, managed to cut off the Austrian defenders of Solferino before taking the town at around 2pm. Following this they managed to roll up the Austrian positions between Solferino and Cavriana, decisively winning the day. The only bright spot for the Austrians was the determined stand made by General von Benedek against the Sardinian assault on San Martino. The Austrians retreated from the battlefield having lost 22,000 casualties, though the Franco-Sardinian losses amounted to 17,000. In the face of this slaughter Napoleon III and Franz Josef agreed an armistice on 7 July that led to the peace of Villafranca.

La Chiesa Ossario di San Pietro in Vincoli stands on the battlefield of Solferino and houses the remains of more than 7,000 soldiers killed during the battle.

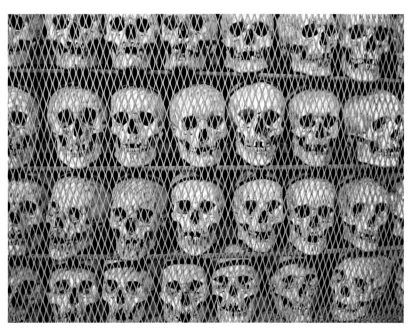

east of Milan known as the Quadrilateral, abandoning the city to the advancing French and Sardinian forces.

Gyulai resigned his command on 18 June and was replaced in command of the reinforced Austrian forces, now split into two armies, by the emperor Franz Josef who resolved to defend the river crossings of the Mincio around the village of Solferino.

The Franco-Sardinian forces advanced towards this position and straight into the Austrians on the morning of 24 June.

The battle itself was a confused affair, as was to be expected when two forces essentially blundered into each other. The Austrians had 130,000 men split between their two armies and against them were 92,000 French and 39,000 Sardinians. Of all the troops involved, the French had a qualitative

The town of San Martino Della Battaglia, only a few kilometres south of Lake Garda. Here the Sardinian troops attempted to drive an Austrian corps under General Von Benedek out of their positions with little success. Now a large memorial is located here, dedicated to King Victor Emmanuel II and the Risorgimento.

Dybbøl

18 April 1864

The battle of Dybbøl of 18 April 1864 saw the settlement of the Schleswig-Holstein question that had plagued Danish and German relations throughout the 19th century. The twin duchies of Schleswig and Holstein had historically formed part of the Danish crown possessions, but had been ruled by a German aristocratic class who more closely associated themselves with the states of the bordering German Confederation. An attempt by the Danish King Frederick VII to incorporate the duchies more firmly into the fabric of Denmark led to the outbreak of the First Schleswig War, which lasted from 1848 until 1851 and pitted Denmark and her allies against the German landowners of Schleswig-Holstein, who were supported by troops from the German Confederation, most notably Prussia. The Prussians had forced the Danish troops out of the twin duchies, but the war had ended inconclusively.

The death of the old Danish King Frederick VII in 1863 brought the issues out in the open again as his successor, Christian IX, felt compelled to sign a new constitution altering the position of Schleswig and Holstein within the federation of Denmark. This outraged the German party in the twin duchies as well as their supporters in the German Confederation. On 24 December 1863 German troops occupied Holstein, while on 16 January 1864 the Prussians, supported

The Dybbøl Mill stands as both a landmark and a memorial. It was destroyed in both Schleswig Wars but always rebuilt afterwards.

by the Austrians, demanded that Denmark repudiate the new constitution, a demand that was rejected. On 1 February 1864 an Austro-Prussian force crossed the border into Schleswig starting the Second Schleswig War.

The Danish Army had already withdrawn from Holstein and taken up positions along the Danevirke, a historic earthwork that stretched across the peninsula. However the Danish commander, General de Meza, feared that as

A Danish memorial stone dedicated to some of the 3,600 dead on their side at the battle.

Walking trails pass through the battlefield and link the many defence systems reaching from the beach up to the top of the hill. Only the memorial stones and remnants of fortifications reveal the landscape's bloody history.

the swampy ground on the flanks of this position had frozen over, the Austro-Prussian forces would be able to outflank him, and on 5 February he withdrew to a further defensive position in trenches around the town of Dybbøl. This town would become the site of the key battle of the war, as the Austro-Prussian forces followed up the Danish retreat and put the town under siege at the beginning of April. Having tried and failed to rush the position, the Austro-Prussian forces set about a systematic siege, finally launching their main attack on 18 April, which quickly took control of the first line of Danish positions. It took a bold counter-attack by the Danish 8th Brigade to hold the attacking German forces back long enough for the remaining Danish forces to withdraw to the island of Als, though at a heavy cost in casualties. By the end of the day the Danes had suffered 3,600 casualties compared to the 1,200 lost by the Austro-Prussian force.

The war dragged on throughout 1864 until the complete loss of the Jutland Peninsula forced the Danes to capitulate in October, with control over Schleswig and Holstein being turned over to Austria and Prussia.

Artillery pieces on top of the hill between the windmill and museum.

The view from the top of the ridge at Dybbøl, close to the windmill, down the southern slope to the waters of the Vemmingbund. This slope held some of the principal Danish fortifications and was thus the scene of some of the heaviest fighting on 18 April 1864.

The Kongeskansen, 'the king's redoubt', a Prussian fortification built on top of the earlier Danish works. It is known as the king's redoubt after King Christian X who held a celebration here for the integration of North Schleswig into Denmark in 1920.

Königgrätz

3 July 1866

The battle of Königgrätz, also known as the battle of Sadowa, was the only major battle during the Austro-Prussian War of 1866. This conflict, ostensibly fought over Prussian intervention in the Austrian-controlled Duchy of Holstein, was more about the future direction that was to be taken by the German Confederation. This grouping of states had risen from the ashes of Napoleon's Confederation of the Rhine after 1815 and contained 39 separate states, of which the two dominant powers were Austria and Prussia. The former sought to retain a loose confederation of states, whilst the latter, under the influence of Count Otto von Bismarck, sought a unified German empire centred upon the Prussian capital of Berlin. When the Prussian intervention in Holstein provoked Austria into war the Emperor Franz Josef aimed both to reconquer his lost territory in Italy, and to partition Prussia and share its territory amongst other states in the German Confederation, reducing it as a rival. However, he underestimated both the ability of the Prussian military, reshaped under its commander Moltke 'the elder', and the speed at which they could operate.

Moltke decided to concentrate his forces on the Austrians in Bohemia, leaving only 50,000 men to cope with Austria's southern German allies,

The village of Chlum. This village had a central role in the battle as it lay behind the centre of the Austrian lines and its capture signalled the collapse of the Austrian position and the start of their retreat across the Elbe.

Bavaria, Baden and Württemberg. He split his main force of some 250,000 men into three separate armies: the First Army under Prince Frederick Charles (93,000), the Second Army under Crown Prince William (115,000), and the Army of the Elbe under Karl Herwarth von Bittenfeld (48,000). An Austrian

it to withdraw across the Elbe and retreat to Vienna. The Austrians lost over 44,000 men in the course of the day, while the Prussians lost 9,000. However, they were too weak to follow up the victory immediately and both sides accepted an armistice on 22 July. The treaty that ensued saw Prussia dissolve the German Confederation, replacing it with a North German Confederation as a unified state consisting of 22 entities – kingdoms, principalities and duchies – with Prussia as its head.

More memorials near Čistěves. The Prussians lost some 9,000 casualties in the battle while the Austrians lost a staggering 44,000. As Austria was not a signatory to the Geneva Convention its medics were unable to remain on the battlefield, causing unnecessary deaths amongst the wounded.

A memorial to the battle located on Route E442 near Čistěves.

Army of 190,000 with 25,000 Saxon allies was mobilizing under General von Benedek to face them.

The three Prussian armies crossed the border and the Second Army began to drive the Austrians before them. Following a series of actions, Benedek withdrew north of Prague towards the river Elbe near the fortress of Königgrätz, and at the same time Moltke moved the First Army and the Army of the Elbe so that they would descend on the Austrian position from the north-west, trapping them. In the event, the First Army and Army of the Elbe arrived on 2 July before the Second Army, which was delayed by dreadful weather conditions. The two Prussian armies, although outnumbered, launched an attack on the Austrian position on the morning of 3 July 1866. The Austrians had rebuffed this attack by 11am, and had Benedek committed his cavalry he could have defeated the weaker Prussian force. However he delayed and this allowed the Prussian Second Army to arrive and attack the flank of the Austrian Army from the north, forcing

An overview of the battlefield of Königgrätz, showing the triangle between Chlum (right, not visible), Čistěves (on the left) and Máslojedy (right background). In the shadow at the left background is the Swiep Forest.

A memorial in the landscape near Máslojedy. To the left a part of the Swiep Forest is visible.

A memorial near Chlum. In the far right background is the modern Czech city of Hradec Králové, as Königgrätz is now called.

Mars-la-Tour and Gravelotte-St-Privat

16–18 August 1870

The twin battles of Mars-la-Tour and Gravelotte-St-Privat trapped the whole of the French Army of the Rhine under Marshal Bazaine in the fortress city of Metz on the French frontier. It remained here until its surrender on 28 October 1870.

The French emperor, Napoleon III, had been provoked into declaring war on Prussia on 19 July over the issue of a Hohenzollern succeeding to the Spanish throne, notably by Otto von Bismarck's release of the 'Ems Telegram' containing an edited account of a meeting between the German king and the French ambassador. The French were utterly unprepared for war and let the initiative slip to the Prussians, who mobilized their troops and assembled them near the French frontier in three separate armies. The French Army of the Rhine, consisting of the pre-war armies of Alsace, Lorraine and Châlons, began to come together under the command of Napoleon III himself between Thionville and Strasbourg. The French began to advance on 31 July, pushing across the border on 2 August and capturing the town of Saarbrücken. However the superior Prussian forces then began a series of counter-offensives that first split Marshal MacMahon's forces off from the main French Army of the Rhine, compelling him to retire to Châlons, and then drove the remainder of the French Army towards the fortifications of Metz.

The Porte des Allemands at Metz. One of the most distinctive features of the city, the Porte des Allemands was originally constructed in the 1230s and had further towers added in the 15th century. Named after a religious order who maintained a hospital nearby, the medieval fortifications were incorporated into Vauban's defences and restored in the late 19th century.

Metz Cathedral standing above the Moselle. The city was heavily fortified during the 17th century by the noted French engineer Vauban, and it was here that the French Army of the Rhine, later renamed the Army of Metz, retired following the battle of Gravelotte-St-Privat.

On 12 August Napoleon III himself replaced MacMahon as commander of the Army of the Rhine and went on to Châlons. He ordered Bazaine to follow him there via Verdun, avoiding any further defeat by the Prussians. However, the Prussian Second Army, leaving the First Army to hold Bazaine in place, had crossed the Moselle to the south and cut off the Metz–Verdun road. At the battle of Mars-la-Tour two Prussian corps, with only 30,000 troops, managed to hold off the 135,000 troops of the French Army of the Rhine for the whole day, gradually being reinforced until by the end of the day there were 95,000 Prussians on the battlefield. The following day the French retired a short way towards Metz, stopping on a series of ridges stretching from the Moselle towards the village of St-Privat.

On the 18th the Prussians, who had now assembled the full force of their First and Second armies, launched a series of attacks on the French position which began at 8am. The Prussian First Army was fed piecemeal into the attack against the French positions, suffering heavy casualties to accurate fire from French rifles and *mitrailleuses*, an early form of machine gun. In the afternoon the Second Army launched the Prussian Guard at the right wing of the French Army around St-Privat and, having suffered heavy casualties, these troops finally broke through with the support of a massive artillery effort. This caused the rolling up of the French position, with IV and VI corps breaking and withdrawing, precipitating the whole of the French Army pulling back to the fortifications of Metz. The casualty figures on the Prussian side were horrendous, with over 20,000 dead and wounded compared to 12,000 for the French; a testament to their unimaginative assault tactics.

The countryside south of the Metz–Verdun road between the villages of Rezonville and Vionville. It was around here on 16 August that the Prussian troops of III and X corps attacked the French Army of the Rhine as it tried to get through to Verdun.

Prussian memorials on the battlefield between Vionville and Rezonville. The Prussians suffered heavy casualties in their headlong attacks on the French centre in the battle of Mars-la-Tour.

Another Prussian memorial. The French Chassepot infantry rifles were a generation ahead of their Prussian counterparts in terms of accuracy and range, though the Prussian artillery was vastly superior to the French.

✛ Sedan

1 September 1870

Following the battles of Mars-le-Tour and Gravelotte-St-Privat in the Franco-Prussian War of 1870, the main French Army of the Rhine became trapped within the fortress city of Metz, unable and unwilling to take any active role in the war. The focus shifted to Châlons, where Marshal MacMahon had retreated with his corps following the battles of the frontiers in early August. Here Napoleon III joined him, and the Army of Châlons was formed out of the remnants of the French troops of V, VII corps, together with the newly formed XII Corps and I Corps. MacMahon decide to advance to the north, heading towards Reims, hoping to avoid the Prussians and eventually link up with Bazaine's forces trapped in Metz. The Prussians had left their First and Second armies to continue besieging Metz and sent the Third Army along with the newly created Army of the Meuse to deal with the last remaining French field army. The two Prussian armies manoeuvred around the outnumbered French force, causing it to fall back towards the city of Sedan, only 11km (seven miles) from the Belgian frontier. On 29 August the two sides met at the battle of Beaumont where the French were beaten, losing 5,000 men, and driven into Sedan itself. Both sides rested on 30 August, and on the 31st the Prussian corps surrounded the French position, cutting off all chance of escape for the beleaguered forces trapped within Sedan. On 1 September the French attempted to break out through the village of Bazeilles, but ran headlong into a Prussian advance that drove them backwards. MacMahon was wounded in this action and control of the army passed to General Ducrot. The Prussians then brought up their artillery and began to wear down the French position. In a last, desperate attempt to break out of the Prussian encirclement the French cavalry launched a series of charges against the village of Floing to the west. However these proved fruitless and only resulted in heavy French casualties.

By 5pm Napoleon III called for an armistice to spare his troops any further suffering and the following day he surrendered the Army of Châlons to the Prussian King, Wilhelm I. The French had lost 17,000 casualties and 21,000 prisoners, while a further 83,000 went into captivity following the surrender. The battle of Sedan proved to be the end for Napoleon III and the Second Empire; his government was overthrown, the Third Republic was proclaimed, and Napoleon III went into exile in Great Britain, dying in 1873. However, the battle of Sedan did not see the end of the Franco-Prussian War, which dragged on for a further five months as Paris held out against a Prussian siege until an armistice was agreed on 27 January. The immediate aftermath of the war saw the proclamation of Wilhelm I as Kaiser of the newly created German Empire in the Hall of Mirrors at Versailles on 1 January 1871, and the peace treaty between the new empire and France saw the loss of the Alsace and Lorraine.

A memorial stone for 500 Bavarians killed in the battle. The inscription reads 'Hier ruhen 500 tapfere Bayern' (Here rest 500 brave Bavarians).

A memorial in the village of Bazeilles to French military and civilian casualties of the battle. The storming of Bazeilles by the Prussians gave rise to rumours of both the Prussians slaughtering civilians and the French arming civilians, both against the accepted rules of war.

The cemetery in Bazeilles hosts both the Prussian and French dead. The village was the scene of hard fighting as the French attempted to break out of the Prussian encirclement and the Prussians sought to destroy the French Army of Châlons.

The northern sector of the battlefield of Sedan, showing the landscape near to the village of Illy – the scene of heavy fighting on 1 September 1870. The wood to the rear is the Bois de la Garenne, where French troops retreated following the Prussian successes.

Ypres
1914–18

The area around the Flemish town of Ypres is renowned for its central role in three major battles of World War I, the battles of First, Second and Third Ypres, and its association with the British Expeditionary Force from 1914 to 1918.

The battle of First Ypres took place following the German withdrawal after the battle of the Marne and the 'race to the sea'. The BEF moved to the left flank of the Allied forces, taking up positions in Flanders where it would remain for the next four years. In doing so it found itself pitted against the German Fourth and Sixth armies under Falkenhayn. The battle began on 20 October 1914, when 14 German divisions attacked along a 32km (20 mile) front. Despite breaking through the Belgian defences to the north they suffered heavy losses, particularly within their war-raised volunteer divisions, who proved no match for the BEF rifles in the central sector. On 24 October, progress was halted when the Belgians blew up the sea dykes, flooding the region. Six German divisions renewed the offensive on a narrower front on 31 October, breaking through Haig's I Corps at Gheluvelt before hastily assembled reinforcements pushed them back. The final offensive came on 11 November with Ypres as its objective, when the German attack failed to crush the resistance of the BEF and the crisis passed.

The battle officially ended on 22 November 1914 as the Allies entrenched themselves along what would become known as 'the Salient', a triangular-shaped projection into the German front line that was to prove an uncomfortable home for British troops over the following years. Amongst the battle's dead were an estimated 41,000 of Germany's ill-prepared volunteer forces, as well as over 58,000 British and Commonwealth forces. The battle of Second Ypres, fought

The Cloth Hall in Ypres. Devastated by the Germans in World World I, it was rebuilt between 1933 and 1967. This building is now home to the In Flanders Fields Museum dedicated to World War I history.

This section of restored trench lies in Bayernwald, or Croonaert Wood to the British, a small copse behind the German front line on the Messines Ridge close to the village of Wytschaete. The trenches are based on original German plans from the mid-war period.

between 22 April and 25 May 1915, is famous as the first occasion that poison gas was used offensively on the Western Front. The German Fourth Army attacked, supported by 160 tons of chlorine gas. This new weapon overwhelmed French forces and the German assault rolled up the line, only to be held up by determined resistance from Canadian forces. Desperate measures were taken to protect the defending troops from the effects of the chlorine, and rudimentary gas masks were rushed to the front. These proved effective enough for the line to be held in most places, though the Allies were forced to withdraw, surrendering the highest ground of the Ypres Salient and losing up to five kilometres (three miles) of ground by the time of the final German gas assault on 25 May 1915.

The largest of the three battles took place from 31 July 1917 and formed Field Marshal Sir Douglas Haig's major offensive of the year. General Hubert Gough's Fifth Army took the principal part in the early battles to the north of Ypres – the battles of Pilckem Ridge, Gheluvelt and Langemarck. Despite some

Remnants from the many battles of the Ypres Salient can be found in the fields themselves. Every year when ploughing, farmers uncover quantities of ordnance used by the various combatant nations fighting on the Western Front. Shells found by farmers are so common that they are simply left in front of their premises to be collected by bomb disposal squads.

initial success, such as the capture of Pilckem Ridge, the Fifth Army became bogged down and, towards the end of August, Haig decided to try again with Plumer's Second Army. Having prepared his men and plans for three weeks, Plumer launched a series of attacks against the Menin Road Ridge and Polygon Wood, culminating in the battle of Broodseinde from 4 October, which finally drove the German defenders from Polygon Wood. At this point the weather once again intervened, with heavy rain making the battlefield impassable.

Haig was still determined to push on and launched his final set of offensives, aimed at securing Passchendaele Ridge on 12 October. On 6 November Canadian troops finally captured the village of Passchendaele, ending the battle. Over 250,000 men had died on each side in terrible conditions, which have since become a byword for the suffering endured by the front-line infantryman in World War I.

The Canadian Memorial at St Julien. The monument commemorates the 18,000 Canadian soldiers who withstood the first German gas attack during the battle of Second Ypres on 22–24 April 1915; 2,000 of them were killed.

This peaceful pond is actually a mine crater filled with water. The battle of Messines Ridge, 7 June 1917, formed a prelude to the main battle of Third Ypres and one of its features was the use of 19 huge mines that destroyed the German front-line position, wiping out 10,000 men in the process. Many of the craters left by those mines are still visible, and this image shows one of the two Kruisstraat Craters.

The modern-day scene of Passchendaele is a long way from the hellish, mud-filled landscape that existed in the autumn of 1917. Today the fields are once more under cultivation. This picture was taken in the middle of the former killing ground. To the right stands the church of Passchendaele village.

Similar to the Somme battlefields, the Commonwealth War Graves Commission (CWGC) cemeteries are part of the landscape. There are more than 150 CWGC cemeteries scattered throughout the area around Ypres. The one in the foreground is Mud Corner, while the one to the rear is Prowse Point Cemetery.

The Dolomites

Prior to the start of World War I, Italy was a member of the Triple Alliance along with Germany and Austria-Hungary, which she had signed in 1882. However, on the outbreak of World War I Italy felt no compulsion to join her allies as neither had been directly attacked. The Italian relationship with Austria-Hungary had been fraught with tension since the foundation of the kingdom of Italy in 1866, and this tension was focused on two areas of Austria-Hungary that Italy felt were rightly hers: the Alpine region of the Trentino, and Istria on the Dalmatian Coast. These territorial disputes had brought Italy and Austria-Hungary close to war on a number of occasions, and when in the course of negotiations Great Britain and France offered Italy the Austro-Hungarian territories she sought, she elected to enter the war on their side, as agreed in the Treaty of London signed in April 1915. Italy declared war on Austria-Hungary on 24 May 1915. The territory between the two competing powers was not geographically suited to modern warfare, dominated as it was by the mountains of the Alps – the Dolomites, Carnic Alps and Julian Alps – with only the area around the river Isonzo proving a suitable area for manoeuvre.

Reconstructed Italian barracks in the south wall of the Piccolo Lagazuoi, a position known as Cengia Martini. The Austrians held the peak of the mountain and the positions below, while the Italians held this ledge in the middle of the south wall, enabling them to fire into the Austrian positions below.

With the declaration of war the Italians advanced on all fronts and the Austrians, who were already heavily committed on the Eastern Front against the Russians, were forced to withdraw, leaving parts of their territory in Italian hands. Some of this territory included the Dolomites, a range of the Eastern

Alps, where the Austro-Hungarians had created a defensive line running through the mountains. The Italians and Austrians found themselves fighting a form of trench warfare thousands of metres above sea level in a harsh and unforgiving

The Tre Sassi fort located at the Valparola Pass, built in 1897, was one of many Austrian fortresses protecting the border with Italy. It was evacuated after being hit by artillery fire in the summer of 1915. It now houses the Museo Della Grande Guerra 1914–1918.

environment. In an effort to move troops, supplies and equipment in this difficult theatre of war the Italians created a network of what became known as *vie ferrate*, or 'iron roads', a series of ropes and ladders fixed to the surface of rocks to assist movement. Mountains, and even glaciers, were tunnelled into in order to create shelters and dugouts, but the extreme winter conditions of 1916 proved perilous for both sides and a large number of soldiers were killed by avalanches and rock falls before any enemy action could take its toll.

Due to the nature of the terrain the Dolomites did not see any great breakthrough by large numbers of soldiers, and the decisive battles of the Italian Front took place to the east along the Isonzo river valley. But the battles for the peaks of the Dolomites and other Alpine ranges remained hard fought until the final armistice with Austria-Hungary was signed on 3 November 1918. The remains of the *vie ferrate* have been upgraded, with metal ladders and steel cables replacing the rickety wooden ladders and ropes used by the troops at the time, and the region is now a major tourist destination famed for its climbing.

The Galleria Lagazuoi was created by the Italians in order to place a mine beneath Austrian positions. It is 1,100m (3,609ft) long and is nowadays one of the principal tourist attractions in the area.

An Austrian observation post on the Hexenstein (Sasso di Stria). The Hexenstein is located at the intersection of the passes of Falzarego and Valparola, and was therefore a position of strategic importance when it came to controlling access to the valleys, as well as a perfect spot for observation in all directions.

A German cemetery on the top of Pordoi Pass. Here lie the remains of 8,582 Austrian and German soldiers of World War I and 847 soldiers from World War II. The Pordoi Pass is the highest pass (2,239m, 7,346ft) accessible by cars in the Dolomites.

The picture shows the Travenanzes Valley near Cortina d'Ampezzo and is one of the most scenic spots in the whole of the Dolomites. Between May 1915 and 1917 this valley was a killing ground as the Austrians held the mountains to the left and the valley itself while the Italians held the famous Tofana mountain range to the right.

The labyrinth of rocks in the Fontana Negra was deadly ground and one of the most surreal of all the battlefields in the Dolomites. The narrow gorge between the 700m high (2,297ft) walls on both sides of Tofana Di Rozes and Tofana Di Mezzo provides access to the Travenanzes Valley below. This ground was occupied by the Austrians until summer 1916, overlooked on three sides by higher Italian positions.

The Isonzo

June 1915–November 1917

When Italy entered the war on the side of the Allies towards the end of May 1915, there were relatively few strategic options for her to pursue. The territory of Italy bordering Austria-Hungary was dominated by the high mountains of the Eastern Alps – unsuitable territory for a major campaign – and the only realistic strategic option open to the Italian commander-in-chief, General Count Luigi Cadorna, was to attack to the north-east across the Isonzo valley, much of which lies in modern Slovenia.

This region is flanked by mountains, but consists of a relatively flat area between the Krn Mountain and the sea, and the Italians planned to break through here near the town of Gorizia before taking control of Trieste and pushing northwards further into the centre of Austria. However, the Austrians also realized that the Isonzo valley was the only realistic avenue of assault and planned their dispositions accordingly, leading to a lengthy series of inconclusive battles. The First Battle of the Isonzo was launched on 27 May, shortly after the Italian declaration of war, and the two Italian armies committed to the assault rapidly came up against strong Austrian defences, which rebuffed their attacks in a manner that set the pattern for the rest of 1915. By the end of the year four

The Mengore Hill situated in the Tomlin Bridgehead was the target of sustained attacks by Italian forces. Today the positions are accessible by a well-marked trail and the original Austrian artillery emplacements can be seen.

separate battles had taken place in an attempt to capture Gorizia, resulting in some 161,000 losses for the Italians and 147,000 for the Austrians.

Following a brief respite over the winter of 1915/16, there were a further five battles of the Isonzo in 1916, including the Sixth Battle of the Isonzo which finally saw the Italians capture of the town of Gorizia and gains of six kilometres along a 24km (15 mile) front. The rest of the action on the Isonzo Front during 1916 was

The Isonzo Valley near Caporetto. The river is supposed to be one of the most beautiful in the Alps due to its unique colour and the way in which its appearance can change from wild to calm.

The Redipuglia military memorial contains the graves of over 100,000 Italian soldiers killed in the battles along the river Isonzo. It also holds the grave of the commander of the Italian Third Army, Emanuele Filiberto, the Duke of Aosta.

inconclusive, but served to wear down both the Austrians and Italians and led the former to call upon their ally Germany for assistance. The year 1917 saw further attempts by the Italians to break through, with the Tenth Battle of the Isonzo seeing Italian troops reach positions only 16km (ten miles) away from Trieste before being pushed back by counter-attacks, and the Eleventh Battle seeing the largest commitment of Italian troops yet. However, they narrowly failed to break the Austrian line and the Twelfth Battle of the Isonzo would see a complete reversal of fortunes. This battle, also known as Caporetto, started on 24 October 1917 and saw the newly formed 14th Austro-German Army under General Otto von Below decisively shatter the Italian lines and overwhelm the Second Army, causing an Italian retreat from the territory they had fought so hard to capture for the previous two years. The headlong retreat did not stop until the line of the river Piave, only 32km (20 miles) north of Venice, and it came perilously close to knocking Italy out of the war altogether. The Allies rushed troops to the Italian front and General Armando Diaz replaced Cadorna, and the front line began to stabilize once more.

The river Isonzo near the town of Tolmin, was the scene of 12 consecutive battles from 1915 through to the end of 1917. It is photographed here looking south to where the Austrian front line crossed the river. Here the Austrians had the only bridgehead on the right-hand side of the river that they kept throughout the entire campaign.

Verdun

February–December 1916

The battle of Verdun, fought between February and December 1916, was, along with the Somme, one of the great battles of 1916 and holds a hallowed place in French and German popular memory, equivalent to the battles of the Somme and Passchendaele for the British.

Verdun, strategically located on the river Meuse, had been a fortified site since antiquity and its defences had most recently been updated in the late 19th century following the Prussian victory in the Franco-Prussian War of 1870. The city was protected by a network of strong forts and other outworks to create a fortified region. The area held out in the face of the German invasion of 1914 and formed a salient in the German lines, overlooked on three sides by German positions and guns.

The German commander, General Erich von Falkenhayn, resolved to launch a major offensive here in order to 'bleed France white'. By attacking such a national symbol, which he argued that the French would not be able to abandon, they would be drawn into an attritional battle in which France's manpower reserves would be ground down until they were compelled to seek a negotiated peace. The assault was scheduled for 12 February, and the German

Fifth Army under Crown Prince Wilhelm and with 1,200 guns was assembled overlooking the city and its fortifications.

Having been delayed by nine days by bad weather, the battle opened on the morning of 21 February with the heaviest artillery bombardment ever seen on the Western Front. The attacking forces, spearheaded by specially trained storm troops, pushed back the overwhelmed French defenders and broke through to

Mémorial De Verdun in Fleury, near Fort Douaumont. Located right in the centre of the battlefield, this memorial hosts a museum containing artefacts and testimonies from both the French and German sides.

The river Meuse runs through the centre of Verdun. The city formed the centre of a fortified region constructed by General Séré de Rivières in the 1870s following France's defeat in the Franco-Prussian War.

one of the centrepieces of the Verdun fortifications on 25 February, Fort Douaumont, which fell to a bold assault by a few German pioneers. However, German losses, particularly among the infantry spearheads, had been high and French reinforcements were rushed to Verdun, including the Second Army under General Henri Pétain who took over the defence. He reorganized the French lines, giving particular emphasis to the artillery concentration, ensured that a steady flow of supplies and reinforcements reached the beleaguered city along the only route in and out, the *Voie Sacrée*, and stabilized the front.

At the beginning of March the Germans switched the point of their attack to the right bank of the Meuse, especially the ridge known as Mort Homme, which finally fell in May. By this stage the process of attrition that Falkenhayn had hoped for was wearing both sides down. In June the Germans launched a further major assault that succeeded in capturing Fort Vaux, while on 1 July they reached

Fort Souville, only five kilometres from Verdun. However, this was the closest they got and from this point on the momentum swung towards the French. The battle of the Somme to the north drew off German reserves while Falkenhayn was relieved and replaced by Hindenburg and Ludendorff. The German Army at Verdun now went on the defensive, and in October the French under General Robert Nivelle launched a counter-offensive that won back the key points of the Verdun fortifications one by one, until by 15 December only the Mort Homme remained in German hands. The battle for Verdun drew to a close, leaving the the French with losses of 377,000 and the Germans 357,000.

A turret of Fort Douaumont, one of Verdun's major fortifications that fell to an assault party of German pioneers on 25 February 1916. By this time, the fort had already been stripped of many of its guns to reinforce other sectors of the front.

The soil around Verdun was pulverized with 20 million shells and large areas of the battlefield have been left uncultivated in what are known as red zones, Zones Rouges. This particular image was taken near Fort Souville, which proved to be the high-water mark of the German advance.

The national French cemetery at Douaumont, photographed from in front of the ossuary looking outwards. The cemetery contains 15,000 graves while the ossuary contains the remains of 130,000 unknown soldiers.

A communication trench preserved near Fort Douaumont. The picture shows that if the foliage and bushes are removed, the moon-like battlefield still exists below.

The ruin of the church in Ornes. Ornes is one of the nine villages that were not rebuilt following the war, the Villages Detruits.

The Somme

1 July–13 November 1916

The battle of the Somme is one of the iconic battles of World War I and the events of its first day are permanently etched into the British psyche. The slaughter of thousands of young volunteers of Kitchener's New Army for very little strategic gain has become a poignant motif for the suffering of the Great War in general.

General Sir Douglas Haig, the commander of the British Expeditionary Force, had originally wanted to launch his major offensive of 1916 in Flanders but was persuaded by the French high command to shift his main effort further south, to the valley of the river Somme, where the junction between the British and French fronts lay. Although this offensive was supposed to be led by the French, the launching of the battle of Verdun in February 1916 meant that pressure was brought to bear on the British both to take the leading role and to bring forward the launch date of their offensive. The decision was taken to launch an attack at the end of June, with the bulk of the attacking forces coming from the British Fourth Army under General Sir Henry Rawlinson. A supporting attack was to be made by three French corps to the south of the river Somme. The attack, which was to be carried out largely by troops who had not taken part in any previous battles, was to be preceded by a seven-day intensive artillery barrage that was designed both to destroy the German wire in front of their trench lines and to annihilate the defending troops. In the event, a lack of heavy guns and the right kind of ammunition combined to ensure that neither objective was achieved and, following a two-day delay for further artillery preparation, the

The Newfoundland Memorial Park, a preserved battlefield with trenches and shell holes. The Newfoundland Government bought the land to preserve it as a memorial to the men of the Newfoundland Regiment who fought and died here. The park includes the British and German front lines with no man's land in between.

British assault went forward on the morning of 1 July 1916 in the face of intact German defences and alert defenders.

The explosion of a number of huge mines under the German front lines heralded the opening of the assault at 7.20am and ten minutes later the British and French troops began clambering out of their trenches and moving across no man's land towards their German objectives. The German defenders, emerging from their strongly built dugouts, manned their machine guns and cut down the advancing infantry in huge numbers. There were isolated successes on the British front, with the 30th and 18th divisions capturing their objectives, while the 36th (Ulster) Division managed to capture the Schwaben Redoubt. Overall, however, the first day was a disaster for the British, who suffered 19,240 officers and men killed and 35,493 wounded – nearly 60,000 casualties in total. In contrast the French, south of the river Somme, achieved all of their first-day objectives.

Although the first day of the Somme remains the most remembered, the battle carried on until November 1916. Battles such as that of Bazentin showed that Rawlinson's Fourth Army was becoming more adept at trench warfare techniques, while the German forces on the front were also being steadily worn down, ensuring that reserves were diverted away from the Verdun offensive, which was one of the aims of the Somme campaign in the first place. The Somme also saw the first use of the tank on the battlefield, with 49 of them being used somewhat ineffectively in the battle of Flers-Courcelette on 15 September.

By the time the battle finished on 13 November, the British and Dominion forces had suffered 419,654 casualties, the French 204,253 and the Germans anything up to 680,000. It had been the most destructive battle in the history of mankind to date.

This unusual red dragon memorial to the 38th (Welsh) Division was placed looking towards Mametz Wood in the 1980s. The division lost over 5,000 casualties during the fight for the wood from 7 to 14 July 1916.

Across the Somme battlefield the horizon is often punctuated by cemeteries, such as this one at Dantzig Alley near Mametz, which contains 2,053 graves, predominantly British. The cemetery is named after a nearby German trench captured on 1 July 1916.

The view from the British front line looking across no man's land towards the German positions near Beaumont-Hamel. The actual German front line was located around the wood on the left side of the picture. The small wood in the middle marks the location of the Hawthorn mine crater, one of the 17 mines exploded by the British on the morning of 1 July 1916. In the middle of the picture the Cross of Sacrifice, part of the CWGC cemetery at Beaumont-Hamel, can be seen.

This image shows the area of the Somme front near La Boiselle. It was this battlefield that the British had to cross on 1 July. The Lochnagar Mine was exploded prior to an attack by the 34th Division that saw the Tyneside Scottish take over 2,400 casualties. The valley in the middle of the photo was known as Sausage Valley at the time.

Bernafay Wood Cemetery, which contains 793 British, 122 Australian, four South African, two New Zealand and one Indian burials. The site of the cemetery was captured by the 9th (Scottish) Division during the assaults of 3–4 July 1916.

Vimy Ridge

9–12 April 1917

Following the cataclysmic battles of Verdun and the Somme in 1916, the Allied high command resolved to break the German front decisively through a combined offensive in 1917. The full weight of the French Army was to fall on the German lines in the Champagne region while the British were to attack to the north around Arras, in an effort both to draw German reserves away from the French sector and to break through the new German defences of the Hindenburg Line. A key part of the battlefield was the high ground of Vimy Ridge that dominated the Scarpe Valley below it. The taking of the ridge was entrusted to the Canadian Corps, part of British First Army, under the command of General Sir Julian Byng.

Preparation for the assault on the ridge was lengthy and comprehensive. A detailed artillery plan was devised that was based around a heavy, 20-day bombardment of the German lines, as well as a detailed counter-battery operation and a complex creeping barrage to protect the troops once the assault was under way. The troops themselves were given full details of the attack plan and rehearsed in all aspects of their role in the assault. Additionally they were to be protected prior to the assault by a series of 12 underground subways that led out into no man's land, protecting them from German shellfire. The British plans for the assault were also aided by the fact that, contrary to their defensive doctrine, the German positions along the ridge did not make great use of defence-in-depth positions, and instead the troops were predominantly based in forward positions.

The reserves were also held a long way from the front line, making it difficult to bring them forwards quickly.

The city of Arras, famous for its large squares and beautiful architecture. Arras is 10km (six miles) south of Vimy and 20km (12 miles) north of the Somme battlefields. It was Arras that formed the centre for the offensive undertaken by the British Third and First armies, of which the assault on Vimy Ridge was part.

At 5.30 on the morning of Easter Monday, 9 April 1917, a series of large mines went off under the German front line and a concentrated artillery barrage opened up, firing a combination of high explosive, smoke and gas shells, while the men of the four divisions of the Canadian Corps began the advance up the hill from their protected subways. The initial advance was extremely successful, with three out of the four divisions reaching their first-stage objectives and only the 4th Canadian Division failing to reach Hill 145, the highest point of the ridge. Further objectives fell throughout the day, including eventually Hill 145, leaving only one major objective outstanding – Hill 120, known as 'The Pimple', to the extreme left of the Canadian line. This network of German trenches and fortified positions was taken by a further series of assaults on the 12th to complete the clean sweep of targets. All the attack's objectives had now been taken and the Canadian and British troops were able to consolidate their positions without any great interference from German counter-attacks. Further to the south the Arras offensive also finished on the 14th, without any breakthrough, while the French offensive in the Champagne region proved extremely costly, sparking a mutiny in French front-line units.

Trenches, preserved in concrete, at the Canadian Memorial Park on Vimy Ridge. These were built by veterans immediately after the end of the war.

The German cemetery at Neuville St Vaast, which contains more than 44,000 graves. The cemetery, located just outside Arras, is the largest German one in France and holds the dead from many battles, from Artois in 1914 through to the Spring Offensives of 1918. The battle of Vimy Ridge is but one of them.

A close up of the twin pillars. Designed by the Canadian sculptor and architect Walter Seymour Allward, the monument took eleven years to build. It was officially unveiled on 26 July 1936 by King Edward VIII.

The Canadian Memorial Park, Vimy. Following the end of World War I a whole section of the Vimy Ridge battlefield was ceded by the French Government in perpetuity to the Canadians to create a memorial park, complete with trenches, pillboxes and other features.

The Cabaret Rouge Cemetery is named after a French café, later destroyed. It gave its name to this sector of the front line. The cemetery contains 7,655 burials, more than half unidentified. Many of the 3,500 Canadians who died in the battle are buried here.

Normandy

6 June 1944

On 6 June 1944 a massive Allied armada arrived off the French coast ready to land its forces on the beaches of Normandy. Four years after they had been forced off the Continent at Dunkirk, the British, now joined by the Americans, Canadians and numerous detachments from occupied countries, were ready to return in force to north-west Europe.

An invasion on this scale required much planning, and the Allied forces involved had been training for the operation from 1943 onwards, with large areas of southern England being turned over to troop training and the stockpiling of supplies, while new weapons and techniques were developed to break the German defences of the Atlantic Wall. At the same time the Germans, aware of the imminent threat, were working hard to improve the quality of their fortifications, and the appointment of Field Marshal Erwin Rommel to oversee the coastal defences gave this process a further impetus.

The Allied plan for the invasion of France, Operation *Overlord*, called for an airborne assault on the night prior to the landings to both sow confusion amongst the defenders and to capture several key tactical features. At the same time a massive invasion fleet, under the command of Admiral Sir Bertram Ramsey, would transport the invasion force across the Channel to the Normandy beaches. The land forces were under the command of General Dwight D. Eisenhower, while the actual invasion was to be carried out by the

21st Army Group under General Bernard Montgomery, which contained the First US and Second British armies. Facing them were the static occupation

The Musée Du Débarquement d'Utah Beach at Sainte-Marie-Du-Mont. The Normandy coast contains many monuments and museums to the invasion and the one on Utah Beach is based around a fortification of German strongpoint WN5.

The Normandy American Cemetery and Memorial at Colleville, above Omaha Beach, contains the graves of 9,387 US servicemen who died on D-Day or during the battle for Normandy that followed.

landing at Utah Beach also went well, with the US troops establishing a solid beachhead. However, Omaha Beach proved a different story. The failure of the supporting armour to reach the shore, combined with an unusually strong German defensive position, left the initial waves of attackers pinned down and trapped under heavy artillery and machine-gun fire. At points the evacuation of the beach was seriously considered and even by the end of the day the US forces had only managed to advance 2,000m (6,562ft). However, the threat of withdrawal had receded and the Allied force had returned to the continent to stay.

Shellholes on top of the Pointe du Hoc. This position, located between Utah and Omaha beaches, was the site of a strong German artillery battery and was a particular target for Allied offshore bombardment and counter-battery fire, as well as severe aerial bombardment.

divisions of the German Army Group B, supported by Panzer units held in reserve.

Following a delay of 24 hours due to poor weather conditions, the invasion started on the night of 5/6 June 1944 with the dropping of three airborne divisions, the US 82nd and 101st and the British 6th, to secure the flanks of the Allied invasion area. The night-time drop caused many problems and the paratroopers and glider troops became widely scattered and suffered heavy casualties; they did, however, occupy many of their objectives and cause widespread confusion in the German rear areas. The main invasion force followed on the morning of 6 June, with the US First Army landing on Utah and Omaha beaches, and the British Second Army assaulting Gold, Juno and Sword beaches. The Anglo-Canadian forces went ashore relatively smoothly, supported by the specialized armour of the 79th Armoured Division, and managed to secure the beaches. However, they failed to capture the key city of Caen behind Sword Beach, which was to cause problems for the rest of the Normandy campaign. The US

The German defences on Omaha Beach were particularly strong and had been manned by experienced troops from the 352nd Division rather than the second-rate troops that were often used for occupation and coastal defence duties.

Utah Beach, shown near the location of the Utah Beach Museum. In contrast to the experience of Omaha Beach, the landings of the US 4th Division on Utah Beach went smoothly, with the division losing 200 men on D-Day itself.

Gold Beach, near the town of Arromanches. In order to bring supplies ashore the Allies constructed artificial harbours that were towed across the Channel in sections and put together on the French side on Gold and Omaha beaches. These Mulberry harbours gave good service until partially wrecked by a major storm from 19 June onwards. The relics seen here are concrete sea defences, designed to protect the harbour structures.

An American memorial dedicated to the 5th Engineer Special Brigade located on top of a bunker from the German strongpoint WN62 above Omaha Beach. This was the strongpoint responsible for pinning down large numbers of US troops on D-Day.

The Easy Red and Fox Green sectors of Omaha Beach, just below German strongpoint WN62. This was one of the bloodiest sections of D-Day as the machine-gunners in the German strongpoint pinned down the attacking forces of the US 1st and 29th infantry divisions.

Operation *Market Garden*

17–25 September 1944

Following the collapse of the German military position in France and Belgium in late August and early September 1944, there was a window of opportunity for an Allied operation to break the German front decisively and push on to the river Rhine. The normally cautious British commander Field Marshal Montgomery devised an ambitious plan for a combined airborne and ground operation that would seize a key bridge over the Rhine at the town of Arnhem. The plan, Operation *Market Garden*, was split into two halves with *Market* consisting of coordinated drops by the British and US divisions of the Allied First Airborne Army to grab control of both the bridge at Arnhem and key river crossings at Eindhoven and Nijmegen, while *Garden*, a ground assault by the British XXX Corps, would break through and relieve the lightly armed airborne forces to secure the vital crossings. German resistance was expected to be weak, and the operation was planned hurriedly to take advantage of the circumstances on the ground.

On the morning of 17 September 1944 the three divisions of First Airborne Army took off for their targets: the British 1st Airborne Division heading for Arnhem itself, the US 101st Airborne Division for Eindhoven and the US 82nd Airborne Division for Nijmegen. At the same time XXX Corps under General Brian Horrocks also advanced, spearheaded by the tanks of the Irish Guards, part of the Guards Armoured Division. The 101st Airborne attack at Eindhoven was the most successful of the three, with most of their objectives achieved by the end of the first day. Further north at Nijmegen the 82nd Airborne captured some of their objectives, but failed to control the key road bridge in the centre

The target of the British 1st Airborne Division, the road bridge across the Rhine in Arnhem, rebuilt after the war to original plans. The bridge is now called 'the John Frostbrug', after John Frost, the commander of the 2nd Battalion that held its northern end until the collapse of the position on 21 September.

The grounds of the Hartenstein Hotel, Oosterbeek. During the battle the hotel was the British divisional headquarters of General Urquhart and now contains the Airborne Museum 'Hartenstein'. It was from here that the final evacuation of the Allied forces was organized.

finally secure the bridge, and the British tanks started crossing on the evening of the 20th. However, this was too late for the isolated 2nd Battalion at Arnhem Bridge who, having held out in the face of overwhelming odds, had run out of water, medical supplies and ammunition, and the position collapsed on 21 September. The rest of the 1st British Airborne Division was encircled in a pocket around the village of Oosterbeek. This position was evacuated on the night of 25/26 September, signalling an end to the operation and the final failure of the plan.

The old town of Nijmegen, which was the objective of the 82nd Airborne Division in its landings of 17 September 1944.

of Nijmegen, while the British at Arnhem were having the most difficulties. They found that their radios were ineffective and that they faced much stronger resistance than expected, and the only troops that managed to reach the bridge in the centre of Arnhem were the 2nd Battalion under Lieutenant-Colonel John Frost. On the ground XXX Corps was finding it tough going. Highway 69, the road along which the advance was channelled, was only two lanes wide and constant attacks by German troops flanking the road caused endless stoppages, ensuring that the corps only moved forwards 11km (seven miles) on the first day of operations. The ground operations went better on the second day, with XXX Corps managing to cover 32km (20 miles), and on the third day they reached the positions of the 82nd Airborne at Nijmegen. However, the vital bridge still lay in German hands. It took an amphibious assault by the 82nd Airborne to

The 1936 road bridge across the river Waal at Nijmegen. Despite being one of the initial targets of the operation, the bridge did not fall until the 20th, causing further delay to an operation that was already running late.

South bank of the Lower Rhine opposite Oosterbeek. On the night of 25/26 September 1944 the remnants of the British 1st Airborne Division were evacuated here during Operation Berlin, *the retreat from Arnhem, supported by troops and artillery from XXX Corps.*

Airborne reinforcements in the form of the 1st Polish Parachute Brigade were dropped near here, a stretch of the Lower Rhine, in the hope of their being able to use the Driel-Heveadorp ferry. However, by the time they arrived the ferry had been destroyed and the north bank was already in the hands of the Germans.

Hürtgen Forest

September 1944–February 1945

Following the successful campaign in Normandy and the Allied invasion of southern France, the German position in Western Europe was in severe danger of collapse. Throughout August and early September 1944 the German Army had been pushed headlong out of its positions in France and Belgium with Allied armies in full pursuit. However, as they approached the German frontier the front began to harden, and nowhere was this more the case than around the positions of the Westwall – known to the Allies as the Siegfried Line – and especially where it ran through the dense groves of the Hürtgen Forest. This was to prove a costly battlefield for the men of the US First Army as they tried to push through to the river Roer in the autumn of 1944.

The first attacks on the Hürtgen Forest were made as part of the attempt to capture the city of Aachen from 16 September onwards, and, although the attempt to break through to the south-east failed, the city was still encircled and, after a month of hard fighting, it finally fell on 21 October. Having taken the city, the plan was for the US First Army under General Courtney Hodges to push on towards the river Roer in an action known as Operation *Queen*. As a preliminary to this operation it was decided to clear the towns of the Hürtgen Forest in order to give the US advance more room to manoeuvre and forestall any possible German counter-attacks from positions in the forest. The main role in this attack was given to the 28th Infantry Division, which went into the forest

on 2 November, replacing the battered 9th Infantry Division that had carried out the earlier attacks. The initial target of the attack was the town of Schmidt, which

The view from the town of Schmidt towards the dams of the river Roer. An important objective of Operation Queen *in late 1944, the lakes are now in the heart of the Nationalpark Eifel.*

on 5 December, with the 83rd Infantry Division replacing the 4th Infantry Division on the 3rd, and by the 7th the forest was largely clear. However the cost had been high indeed, with First Army losing 23,000 dead, wounded, captured or missing and an additional 8,000 non-battle casualties from the four divisions involved. The launch of the German Ardennes offensive on 16 December closed down all operations along the Roer, as every effort was made to contain the German threat to the south.

Sunset in the Eifel region. The dense woods and hilly ground proved to be a formidable natural barrier for the highly mechanized troops of the US First Army. The wet autumn of 1944 also ensured that the US advance could not be supported with the level of air power that the Allies had come to expect throughout the campaign in north-west Europe.

'Dragon's teeth' anti-tank fortifications near Simmerath, part of the original Siegfried Line fortifications based around the village. Many of the fortifications of the Westwall were destroyed in the post-war period, but some have survived and many were preserved as museums and memorials.

was captured on the 3rd but immediately recaptured by the Germans. Fighting continued around the town until 10 November, with the 28th Division suffering severe casualties. Both the terrain and weather favoured the defenders, with the US forces' quantitative and qualitative superiority in air power and artillery – as well as their greater numbers of armoured vehicles and troops – all negated by the densely packed woods and inclement weather.

Despite the heavy losses suffered, further assaults were planned through the forest as part of Operation *Queen* itself, with the US 4th Infantry Division attacking on 16 November and suffering a similar fate to its predecessors. On the 20th another division, the 8th Infantry, was committed to the battle and this, combined with a greater number of armoured units committed, saw the US troops begin to make progress. Hürtgen itself fell on 28 November, Bergstein

Fresh snow in the Kall Ravine near the village of Simonskall. The Kall Ravine was the scene of heavy fighting in early November as the 28th Infantry Division attempted to fight its way through to Schmidt. The only supply route ran along the ravine and the difficulties in keeping it open in the face of German counter-attacks can easily be imagined.

A German military cemetery, containing more than 2,300 graves, near the village of Vossenack. Although the battle of Hürtgen Forest is remembered for its high US casualties, the German Army also suffered heavily for its stubborn defence of the region.

The Battle of the Bulge

16 December 1944–16 January 1945

The Battle of the Bulge, which lasted from December 1944 through to January 1945, was the last major offensive in the west, launched through the Ardennes in an attempt to split the two Allied army groups and drive a wedge between the Anglo-American forces both militarily and politically. Despite early operational successes, the operation was overly ambitious and merely served to wear down Germany's last significant armoured reserve.

Following the collapse of their position in Normandy and the Allied invasion of southern France, the Germans had conducted a headlong retreat to the Belgian and German borders where, in what became known as the 'miracle of the west', they managed to stabilize the front following the failure of the Allies' Operation *Market Garden* in September 1944. This led Hitler to decide to launch a major assault on the Allied armies from the heavily wooded Ardennes area with the aim of driving through to Antwerp, splitting the Anglo-American forces in two and encircling four Allied armies behind the German lines. Hitler believed, in the face of opposition from his senior commanders, that such a bold operation, codenamed 'Watch on the Rhine', would allow him to negotiate a peace settlement in the west, leaving his forces free to concentrate on the Soviet threat to the east.

To conduct such a major operation, the German plan called for three armies to launch simultaneous operations against the lightly defended Ardennes

region. These armies were, from north to south, the Sixth Panzer Army, Fifth Panzer Army and Seventh Army. The bad weather of that time of year had grounded aircraft, negating the overwhelming Allied air power, while strict

The Bois Jacques near Foy, north-east of Bastogne. This wooded area formed part of the perimeter defence of Bastogne and was held by E Company of the 506th PIR, 101st Airborne Division, a unit made famous by the book and television series Band of Brothers.

The American Cemetery at Hamm near the city of Luxembourg contains the grave of the commander of the US Third Army, General Patton. He was buried here following his death in a car accident in December 1945.

The Mardasson Hill American Memorial in Bastogne. The star-shaped building, built in 1950, honours the American dead of the battle. Both the memorial and its accompanying museum draw many tourists to Bastogne.

radio discipline left the Allies unable to intercept intelligence and unaware of where and when the major attack was to fall.

At 5.30am on 16 December 1944 the Germans started their assault, with Sixth Panzer Army attacking the Losheim Gap and the Elsenborn Ridge, and the Fifth Panzer Army the Schnee Eifel; the Seventh Army was mainly to push across the river Our and then hold the southern flank of the operation. The Sixth Panzer Army was straightaway held up by pockets of resistance from the two US infantry divisions, 2nd and 99th, and the spearhead of the armoured assault, Kampfgruppe Peiper, was eventually forced to abandon its vehicles and retreat on 23 December after running out of fuel and being surrounded by counter-attacking US forces. They had, however, committed one of the infamous atrocities of the campaign when they shot 77 US prisoners of war in Malmédy on 17 December.

Further to the south Fifth Panzer Army had more success and, despite being held up by a staunch US defence around St Vith, spearhead units

pushed past the town of Bastogne, isolating the 101st US Airborne Division and other units there, before advancing to within 6km (four miles) of the Meuse by 24 December.

By this point the strategic initiative was returning to the Allies, as the German attacking forces were unable to stick to their rigorous timetables and achieve their targets. General Patton's Third US Army started attacking from the south on 19 December and relieved the defenders of Bastogne on the 26th. Despite further German attacks on 1 January 1945 by the Luftwaffe against Allied airfields and German forces in the Colmar Pocket, the Allied forces began operations on 3 January on both sides of the 'bulge' projecting into their lines, eradicating it by 16 January.

The operation had been enormously costly for both sides, with US forces suffering 80,987 casualties and the Germans 84,834. However, on 12 January the Red Army launched a major offensive in the east, to which the Germans no longer had the reserves to adequately respond.

An original German Tiger II tank displayed in front of the museum in La Gleize. It is tank number 213, part of Kampfgruppe Peiper from 1st SS-Panzer Division 'Leibstandarte Adolf Hitler', which was abandoned near the town.

The Hasselpath wood next to Rocherath-Krinkelt in the northern sector of the battlefield. This area saw what is known as the Battle of the Twin Villages as German forces of Sixth Panzer Army sought to drive out the inexperienced 99th Infantry Division and the battle-hardened 2nd Infantry Division. Since 2000 this area has been preserved as a memorial to the fighting that took place here.

The Belgian-German border near Neuhof, one of the spots where the initial attacks of the Battle of the Bulge were launched. It was from here that the 12th SS-Panzer Division pushed forwards heading for Rocherath-Krinkelt on 16 December 1944.

Mist along the Elsenborn Ridge near the village of Wirtzfeld. The ridge was held throughout the battle by the 1st, 2nd and 99th infantry divisions, preventing any German breakthrough at this point.

Seelow Heights

16–19 April 1945

The Seelow Heights were the last serious defensive barrier between the advancing Soviet armies and Berlin in April 1945, and the battle for control of these positions would lead to control of the approaches to the German capital itself. In January 1945 the Soviet armies on the Eastern Front had launched a major offensive from their positions along the Vistula River. This offensive, which involved five Soviet fronts, drove westwards through Poland, capturing Warsaw and pushing on to the river Oder, while at the same time turning northwards into East Prussia and devastating the region. By the time the final German stronghold of Königsberg fell on 9 April, the focus had already shifted back to the west, where the Soviet armies were massing for the final assault on Berlin. On 1 April Stalin had decreed that the operation, codenamed Operation *Berlin*, should begin on 16 April with the aim of reaching the Elbe by the May Day holiday. The Soviet forces were organized with Marshal Zhukov's 1st Belorussian Front opposite the Seelow Heights, with Koniev's 1st Ukrainian Front further south. The main attack was to be supported by Rokossovsky's 2nd Belorussian Front to the north. Opposing them were the German defenders of Army Group Vistula under the command of General Henrici, whose principal units included Third Panzer Army and Ninth Army, which was supported by Fourth Panzer Army to the south. Henrici realized that the most likely Soviet attack route would be along the Berlin autobahn that ran straight through the

Seelow Heights, and he constructed a triple defence line to fortify this position, thinning troops out of the front line to create a defence in depth and blunt the

Soviet artillery, a Katyusha rocket system and a T-34 tank preserved as memorials to the battle on the Seelow Heights. Soviet superiority in artillery and armour would prove decisive in the battle.

Soviet attacks. He also ordered the flooding of the Oder plain in order to further reduce the mobility of the Soviet armoured forces.

On 16 April the Soviet fronts launched their attack, with Zhukov's 1st Belorussian Front assaulting the Seelow Heights head on, following a major artillery barrage and supported by 140 searchlights to both blind the defenders and illuminate the way ahead for the attackers. The assault immediately ran into problems, as the attacking troops became bogged down in the sodden ground and suffered enormous casualties. Although they managed to clear the first line of German defences, Zhukov was compelled to commit his two reserve Guard Tank Armies in order to keep the attack going. To the south, Koniev's attack was proving more successful and his forces crossed the river Neisse and began to put Fourth Panzer Army under pressure. Zhukov regrouped his forces and pushed on the following day, though he was still unable to break the German lines. However the pressure exerted by Koniev on Fourth Panzer Army was causing the two German army groups to separate, rendering their positions untenable. Following further hard fighting on the 18th, the German front finally collapsed on the 19th with the 8th Guards Army under General Chuikov, the hero of Stalingrad, breaking through the third defence line. The way to Berlin now lay open for the Soviet armies.

The river Oder marks the border between modern-day Poland and Germany for a length of 162km (100 miles). Painted concrete columns on the west bank, such as the one shown here, mark German territory.

1941
1945
ВЕЧНАЯ СЛАВА ГЕРОЯМ
ПАВШИМ В БОЯХ
С ФАШИСТСКИМИ
ЗАХВАТЧИКАМИ
ЗА СВОБОДУ
НЕЗАВИСИМОСТЬ
СОВЕТСКОГО
СОЮЗА

A Soviet memorial and museum on the Seelow Heights. Immediately after the war ended, Marshal Zhukov instructed the architect Lew Kerbel to design memorials at Küstrin, Seelow and Berlin.

The hills of the Seelow Heights, rising some 48m above the Oder Valley below, formed the principal defensive barrier on the road to Berlin. This view from the heights near Dolgelin towards the Oderbruch looks over the road from Dolgelin to Sachsendorf, which was one of the main Soviet objectives on 16 April 1945.

The gently sloping heights near Mallnow in the spring. The three consecutive lines of German fortified positions on the heights managed to hold up the Soviet 1st Belorussian Front for three days before sheer weight of numbers ensured that they broke through, having suffered heavy casualties in the process.

Visiting the Battlefields

Alesia, September 52 BC

The village of Alise-Sainte-Reine, in Burgundy, 70km (43 miles) south of Dijon, is widely accepted as the location of the battle. A large MuséoParc that will cover both the battle of Alesia and the wider subject of Gallo-Roman history and archaeology opens in 2011. Until then it is possible to see the impressive statue of Vercingetorix erected by Napoleon III on Mont Auxois, as well as the remains of the later Gallo-Roman town, which are open daily from mid-March to mid-November.

www.alesia.com

Poitiers, 10 October AD 732

The site of the battle of Poitiers is believed to be located near the village of Moussais-le-Bataille, a few kilometres south of the industrial city of Châtellerault. A giant chessboard explains the events of the battle and is open all year round.

www.tourisme-vienne.com

Hastings, 14 October 1066

The modern town of Battle in East Sussex developed around Battle Abbey, founded by William to commemorate the battle. The town contains a small museum while the Abbey itself is run by English Heritage and holds a major exhibition on the battle of Hastings.

www.english-heritage.org.uk

Marchfeld, 26 August 1278

The site of the battle is located near the modern villages of Dürnkrut and Jedenspeigen in Lower Austria, some 50km (31 miles) to the north-east of Vienna. The battlefield itself is marked by a memorial stone, while arms and armour from the period are displayed in the castle of Dürnkrut.

Agincourt, 25 October 1415

The battlefield lies near modern-day Azincourt, 75km south-east of Calais. The Centre Historique Médiéval (www.azincourt-medieval.com) contains many displays and can also provide audio guides for a tour of the battlefield itself. It is open every day except Christmas Day and New Year's Day; closed Tuesdays from November to March.

Murten, 22 June 1476

The town of Murten, around which the battle took place, is one of the prettiest in Switzerland and is situated in the canton of Friburg. The battle is commemorated in the Lake Murten Museum, which is located on the shores of the lake and is open from April to October.

www.museummurten.ch

Nieuwpoort, 2 July 1600

Nieuwpoort lies in the Flanders region of Belgium. The battle of 1600 is marked by the Prince-Mauritzpark, a municipal garden, while all throughout the town are memorials to the events of 1914–18, including the King Albert I Memorial which was constructed in 1938.

Lützen, 14 November 1632

Modern-day Lützen is a small town situated 20km south-west of Leipzig. The battle, and particularly Gustavus Adolphus, is marked by the Gustavus Adolphus memorial site, which contains a chapel built in 1906 and a museum that was opened in 1994 on the 400th anniversary of his birth.

Fehrbellin, 28 June 1675

The Prussian victory at Fehrbellin, a small town 60km (37 miles) north-west of Berlin, is commemorated by the Hakenberg Victory Column, erected between 1875 and 1879, which is 36m (118ft) tall and has a viewing platform at the top.

Vienna, 12 September 1683

Although much changed since the events of 1683, Vienna still contains many of the principal landmarks that existed during the siege, such as the Schweizerhof and St Stephen's Cathedral. The history of the siege is also well covered by the Vienna Museum.

www.wienmuseum.at

Blenheim, 13 August 1704

The only memorial to the battle at the village of Blindheim in modern Bavaria is an inscription on the wall of the church. The battle is also commemorated at the palace of the same name, constructed after the battle in Woodstock, Oxfordshire, UK. This still remains the seat of the dukes of Marlborough and contains many mementoes of the battle.

www.blenheimpalace.com

Gadebusch, 9 December 1712

The village of Gadebusch has a museum in the castle dealing with the history of the area, with an special focus on the battle. Its opening hours are as follows: Closed Mondays. May–October: open Tue–Fri 10–5, Sat/Sun 2–5. November–April: open Tue–Fri 10–4, Sat 2–4; Sun by prior arrangement.

Leuthen, 5 December 1757

The village of Leuthen where the battle took place in now the Polish village of Lutynia, some 16km (ten miles) west of Breslau. There is a memorial on the Schönberg, raised by the German VI Corps prior to World War I, along with another memorial in the south wall of the village church.

Valmy, 20 September 1792

The focal point of the battlefield of Valmy is the windmill, rebuilt in 2005 following its destruction in a storm in 1999. Nearby stands the Kellermann Memorial, built to the memory of the French general in 1892, while a pyramid beneath it holds a lead casket containing his heart.

Austerlitz, 2 December 1805

The battlefield of Austerlitz lies just to the west of the Czech town of Slavkov u Brna, some 10km (six miles) south-east of Brno. The town and battlefield contain a number of memorials, the most impressive of which is the Peace Memorial constructed on the Pratzen Heights and representing all the nations involved; there is also a small museum located there.

Jena and Auerstedt, 14 October 1806

The battlefield of Jena lies just outside the city of the same name on the river Saale in central Germany. There is a museum containing artefacts from the battle on the battlefield itself, the 1806 Jena/Cospeda Museum, while further material on the twin battle of Auerstedt is held in Auerstedt Castle.

www.jena1806.de

Leipzig, 16–19 October 1813

The dominant feature of the battlefield of Leipzig is the Völkerschlachtdenkmal, the Monument to the Battle of Nations, which stands roughly where Napoleon's command post was during the battle. It is 91m (289ft) high and has a viewing platform on top giving impressive views of Leipzig and the surrounding area. There is also a museum, Forum 1813, based around the monument.

www.schillerhaus-leipzig.de

Waterloo, 18 June 1815

In the years following the battle the Lion Mound, a 43m (141ft) high raised hill with a statue of a lion on top, was constructed by William I of the Netherlands to mark the spot where his son was wounded. In recent years an effort has been made to preserve and restore the pivotal farm of Hougoumont and set it up as a visitor centre for the battlefield.

Solferino, 24 June 1859

The village of Solferino lies some 12km (seven miles) south-east of Lake Garda and houses a number of monuments to the battle of 1859. The ossuary is in the old parish church of St Peter and contains over 7,000 skeletons, while a museum stands between the ossuary and the village itself and the Spia d'Italia, a 23m (75ft) high medieval tower west of the village, also contains relics of the battle.

www.solferinoesanmartino.it

Dybbøl, 18 April 1864

The history centre at Dybbøl is based in the remaining Danish fortifications from the period and contains multimedia exhibits detailing the history of the battle and soldiers' experiences. There are a number of re-enactments throughout the year, particularly on the anniversary of the battle when there is also a memorial service.

www.1864.dk

Königgrätz, 3 July 1866

The battlefield of Königgrätz is located near to what is now the Czech city of Hradec Králové. The main part of the battlefield is located around the village of Chlum, some 7km (four miles) from Hradec Králové and this is where the principal battlefield museum is located. A re-enactment of the battle is held every year at the beginning of July.

www.chlum1866.cz

Mars-la-Tour and Gravelotte-St-Privat, 16–18 August 1870

The battlefields of Mars-la-Tour and Gravelotte-St-Privat are both situated in the French department of the Moselle in the east of the country. At present, a large museum detailing the battles of the Franco-Prussian War of 1870 and the annexation of the provinces of Alsace and Lorraine is under construction on the site of the communal museum of Gravelotte. This is scheduled to open in 2009/10. The nearby city of Metz also contains a number of sites associated with the war.

Sedan, 1 September 1870

The battlefield at Sedan in the department of the Ardennes is home to a large number of memorials and museums, particularly in the villages of Floing and Bazeilles, which contains the Last Cartridge House Museum and a cemetery with an ossuary holding the bones of 3,000 French soldiers from 1870. The castle within the city of Sedan itself, although predominantly a medieval structure, also contains artifacts from the Franco-Prussian War.

Ypres, 1914–18

The city and salient of Ypres contains a large number of cemeteries maintained by the Commonwealth War Graves Commission – for a complete list of their sites see www.cwgc.org. The town of Ypres itself contains the In Flanders Fields Museum, located on the second floor of the Cloth Hall, while there is also the Memorial Museum in Passchendaele itself.

www.passchendaele.be

www.inflandersfields.be

The Dolomites, 1915–18

The Dolomites region of the Alps above Lake Garda is a popular destination for tourists engaged in winter sports and other activities. Some of the *vie ferrate* have been restored and upgraded and are now popular with mountain climbers. There is also a series of open-air museums in the Lagazuoi 5 Torri area.

www.dolomiti.org

The Isonzo, June 1915–November 1917

The majority of the region covered by the Italian Isonzo Front now falls in modern Slovenia and the fortifications and memorials in this area are maintained by the Walks of Peace in the Soča Region Foundation (the Soča is the Slovenian name for the Isonzo). Full details of the locations can be found on their website.

www.potimiruvposocju.si

Verdun, February–December 1916

The area around Verdun in the department of the Meuse contains numerous French and German memorials and cemeteries, the most impressive of which is the National French cemetery and ossuary at Fort Douaumont, one of the principal defensive works of Verdun. This contains the remains of over 130,000 French soldiers who died at Verdun and also houses a museum and audio-visual presentation on the battle.

www.verdun-douaumont.com/

The Somme, 1 July–13 November 1916

As with the Ypres salient, the list of British and Commonwealth cemeteries and memorials on the Somme is long, so please see www.cwgc.org for more details. The most impressive is certainly the Luytens-designed Thiepval Memorial. There are also two large museums in the area, the Museé des Abris in Albert and the Historial de la Grande Guerre in Péronne.

www.musee-somme-1916.eu

www.historial.org

Vimy Ridge, 9–12 April 1917

Vimy Ridge is today dominated by the Canadian National Vimy Memorial situated on Hill 145, one of the most fought-over parts of the battlefield, which forms part of a Canadian National Historic Site that stretches over the ridge. The site includes a visitor centre and preserved trenches, including one of the subways used in the attack.

www.vac-acc.gc.ca/remembers/sub.cfm?source=memorials/ww1mem/vimy/battle

Normandy, 6 June 1944

The Normandy coastline is studded with memorials and museums to the events of D-Day. The largest US memorial is the Normandy American Cemetery and Memorial in France, located on the site of the temporary American St Laurent Cemetery, while the principal British cemetery is the Bayeux War Cemetery, which is the largest World War II Commonwealth cemetery in France. Major museums are located in Caen, Arromanches and at Pegasus Bridge.

www.normandy1944.com

www.memorial-caen.fr

Operation Market Garden, 17–25 September 1944

Both Arnhem and Nijmegen have museums dedicated to the liberation of Holland in World War II and Operation *Market Garden*. The Museum of National Liberation is located in Grossbeek just outside of Nijmegen, while the Airborne Museum 'Hartenstein' is situated in the old Hartenstein Hotel, Oosterbeek, which was the headquarters of the British 6th Airborne Division during the battle.

www.bevrijdingsmuseum.nl

www.airbornemuseum.com

Hürtgen Forest, September 1944–February 1945

The most permanent reminders of the fighting around the Siegfried Line in the autumn of 1944 are the surviving defences of the line itself, and remnants exist in a number of sites. There is a small museum in the town of Vossenack, The Hürtgen Forest in 1944 and in Peacetime Museum, while the town also contains a large German cemetery and memorial.

www.westwallmuseum-irrel.de

www.huertgenwald.de/index.php?go=tourismus&forest2&0

The Battle of the Bulge, 16 December 1944–16 January 1945

As expected with such a major campaign, the Battle of the Bulge is well served with museums in the Ardennes region. The December 1944 Historical Museum is situated in the northern part of the battlefield in La Gleize, while the Ardennen Poteau '44 Musuem houses a large collection of period vehicles. In Bastogne there is a proliferation of memorials and museums, of which the most impressive is the Bastogne Historical Center. The National Military History Museum in Diekirch in Luxembourg is also devoted to the campaign.

www.december44.com

webplaza.pt.lu/flener/Poteau_news-text.html

www.bastognehistoricalcenter.be

www.luxembourg.co.uk/NMMH/

Seelow Heights, 16–19 April 1945

The villages of the Seelow Heights are full of memorials and cemeteries dating from the fighting in April 1945. There is a Soviet memorial based around a T-34/85 tank in the village of Kienitz, while a further memorial is located in the village of Seelow itself and a large Soviet cemetery is at the base of the Reitwein Spur.

Index